PRESENTED TO:

....

FROM:

....

DATE:

....

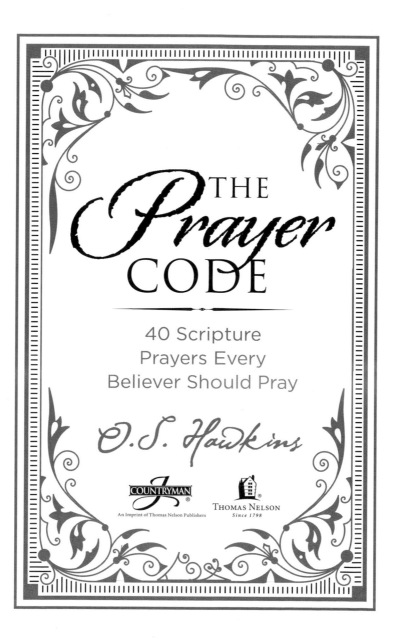

THE
Prayer
CODE

40 Scripture Prayers Every Believer Should Pray

O. S. Hawkins

COUNTRYMAN®

An Imprint of Thomas Nelson Publishers

THOMAS NELSON
Since 1798

Published in Nashville, Tennessee, by Thomas Nelson. Thomas Nelson is a registered trademark of HarperCollins Christian Publishing, Inc.

Thomas Nelson titles may be purchased in bulk for educational, business, fund-raising, or sales promotional use. For information, please email SpecialMarkets@ThomasNelson.com.

Any internet addresses, phone numbers, or company or product information printed in this book are offered as a resource and are not intended in any way to be or to imply an endorsement by Thomas Nelson, nor does Thomas Nelson vouch for the existence, content, or services of these sites, phone numbers, companies, or products beyond the life of this book.

ISBN 978-1-4002-2929-1 (HC)
ISBN 978-1-4002-2927-7 (audiobook)
ISBN 978-1-4002-2928-4 (eBook)

Printed in China

21 22 23 24 25 DSC 10 9 8 7 6 5 4 3 2 1

CONTENTS

Introduction vii

1. A Prayer of Affection 1

2. The Model Prayer 6

3. God-Honoring Prayer 11

4. The Trinity and Prayer 16

5. Prayer According to the Will of God 21

6. Our Prayer Partner 26

7. A Tale of Two Prayers 32

8. A Prayer for a New Beginning 37

9. True Confession 42

10. Prayer and Revival 47

11. Making the Ask 52

12. The Prayer of Jabez 57

13. The Prayer That Gets Results 62

14. Praying Through the Tabernacle 67

15. A Prayer for Service 72

16. Just a Call Away 77

17. A Prayer of Desperation 82

18. A Prayer of Rejoicing 87

19. Prayer and the Harvest 92

20. Listen to Him 97

21. The Pattern of Prayer 103

22. The Original Lord's Prayer 109

23. Praying with Power 114

24. What Happens When People Pray? 120

25. A Prayer for Direction 125

26. God Is Listening 130

27. First Things First 135

28. Put on the Gospel Armor 140

29. Prayer Is the Battlefield of the Christian Life 145

30. Praying for the Sick 150

31. The Prayer That Avails Much 156

32. Prayer and Fasting 161

33. Praying for the Lost 166

34. Answered Prayer 172

35. A Prayer of Acknowledgment 177

36. Prayer and the Will of God 182

37. Watch and Pray 187

38. Prayers from the Cross 192

39. A Prayer of Affirmation 198

40. The Last Prayer of the Bible 204

Epilogue 209

Mission:Dignity 211

About the Author 213

INTRODUCTION

*P*rayer, simply defined, is talking to God. Like all communication, it involves two-way conversation, listening, and speaking. Throughout the sixty-six books of our Bibles, there are over 650 different recorded prayers. Among them are prayers of penitence, prayers of praise, prayers of petition, prayers for protection, and prayers for provision. From the longest prayer—Jesus' high intercessory prayer consuming the entire seventeenth chapter of John's gospel—to the shortest prayer, Peter's desperate plea—"Lord, save me" (Matthew 14:30)—we find prayers from men and women from all walks of life in all types of real-life situations. From the first recorded prayer in the Bible, involving God's conversation with Adam and Eve in the garden of Eden (Genesis 3:8–9), to the last prayer in the Bible, John's plea from Patmos, "Even so, come, Lord Jesus" (Revelation 22:20), we find prayers to emulate no matter what our present needs may be today.

Prayer is the battlefield of the Christian life. Many believers clothe themselves with all the armor Paul described in Ephesians 6:11–17. That is, we wear the helmet of salvation, we hold the shield of faith, we effectively use the sword of the Spirit, which is the Word of God. We get all dressed for the battle, but many of us do not know where the battle is being fought. The very next verse tells us: "Praying always with all prayer and supplication in the Spirit" (v. 18). Again, prayer is the battlefield of the Christian life, the place where the struggles of life are won. It is impossible to win a war if we do not know where the battle is being fought.

It is fascinating that the only thing the disciples ever asked Jesus to teach them to do was to pray. They never asked Him to teach them to preach, or heal, or evangelize, or organize. They had watched His every move for almost three years and knew the secret of His life was in the place of prayer. At times He went up into the mountains and prayed all night. Often, they watched as He arose before daylight to pray. He prayed before every great undertaking. He prayed after each significant achievement. The busier His life became, the more we find Him isolating Himself in the secret place of prayer. Thus, the only thing His faithful followers asked of Him was "Lord, teach us to pray" (Luke 11:1).

In this book we're making the same request in our time: "Lord, teach us to pray." As we journey through these pages, we will find a pattern of prayer helping to lead us through our own time of calling on Him ourselves. *The Prayer Code* is not simply some analytical attempt to study prayer but an examination of people in Scripture who beat out these principles on the anvil of personal experience in order for us to apply these time-tested prayer principles in our own daily lives.

It is now time to begin the journey of unlocking forty Scripture prayers every believer should pray. *The Prayer Code* is written in the same vein as many of the preceding Code books. After each reading you will find a Code Word that will help you remember and live with the truth of the chapter each and every day. Write it down. Keep it with you throughout your day. You will also find a Prayer Promise that you can claim for your very own each day. So, let's begin the journey by making this ancient and earnest request our very own: "Lord, teach us to pray."

1   A PRAYER OF AFFECTION

"Our Father . . ."

—MATTHEW 6:9

How many times have those two words escaped your lips over the years of your own Christian experience? Hundreds? Thousands? They have become so familiar that we often rush through and skip over them in our quest to get to the more direct requests of this model prayer—"Give us . . . forgive us . . . deliver us." But take a step back for just a moment and think on those words—"Our Father." No matter who we might be, whether we have just begun the faith journey or have been walking this path for decades, we can all begin our prayer time with this foundation of true prayer—"Our Father."

I remember the day when I made the marvelous discovery, as a new believer, that I did not have to enter into prayer as some beggar cowering down at the back door, begging for a handout. I am God's own child and seated at His own table. This gives me confidence and even boldness to approach Him. Before we rush once again into the repetition of our Lord's Prayer, let's pause just a moment at these first two words.

AN UNSELFISH RECOGNITION

The foundation of true prayer is *built on an unselfish recognition*. He is *our* Father. In fact, a careful reading of this model prayer reveals the repeated use of these plural pronouns— *our* and *us*. So often we approach the Lord in prayer with a string of "I, I, I" or "me, me, me" or "my, my, my." When we pray as Jesus taught us, there are no singular pronouns, only plural ones. He is not just "My" Father; He is "Our" Father. To my earthly family I am an only child, but in the family of God there is no such thing.

> To my earthly family I am an only child, but in the family of God there is no such thing.

When we pray, "Our" Father, we are acknowledging that we are a part of a big family. Some are different in doctrine, race, culture, or social standing. But the family includes all believers. I have prayed this prayer in countries where believers were under intense persecution or where they were dominated by caste systems, in Africa in open-walled churches under tin roofs, with Arab believers in Muslim countries, in Cuba with those still oppressed by a failed communist regime, in Israel with Jewish believers, and with my Black and Hispanic brothers and sisters in America. Saints in prayer all appear as one. This is what Jesus prayed for us in His high intercessory prayer when He prayed, ". . . that they all may be one . . . that the world may believe that You sent Me" (John 17:21).

The next time you pray this prayer commonly known as the Lord's Prayer, stop at this first word and remember all that is behind it. He is "Our" Father. When we say, "Our Father," we are acknowledging that the true brotherhood of man is really in the family of God. This is the foundation of our praying, for true prayer is built on this unselfish recognition.

AN UNSHAKABLE RELATIONSHIP

When we say, "Our Father," we take a step further to acknowledge that the foundation of true prayer is also *based on an unshakable relationship.* The only way we can refer to Him as "Father" is if we have been born into His family. Many have the erroneous idea that we are all God's children. We are not. We are all God's creations, but we are not all God's children. The Bible is plain on this point. John said, "As many as received Him, to them He gave the right to become children of God" (John 1:12). Paul, inspired by the Holy Spirit wrote, "You are all sons of God through faith in Christ Jesus" (Galatians 3:26). It is plain. Only those who have put their faith in Christ alone and have been born again into His forever family can pray, "Our Father."

As we read the Gospels, we discover that Jesus used the

word *Father* dozens of times in prayer. There is only one occurrence in the New Testament when He prayed without the use of this word. It was on the cross. Three times Jesus prayed from that instrument of execution from which He hung. The first time, "Father, forgive them" (Luke 23:34). The final time, "Father, into Your hands I commit My spirit" (Luke 23:46). But in between those two prayers, when darkness enveloped the earth, when He was bearing our own sin in His own body, is the only time He refrained from using the word *Father*. He cried out, "My God, My God, why have You forsaken Me?" (Matthew 27:46). In the act of bearing the sins of the world, He was separated from the Father so that we might be enabled and empowered to pray based on an unshakable relationship—"Our Father."

All true prayer is built on an unselfish recognition. He is *our* Father. And it is based on an unshakable relationship. He is our *Father*. These two words we have repeated for most of our lives form the very foundation of all our prayers. If we have come to Christ in faith, we are part of a large family and are God's own children, born again by faith in Him. So the real question is this: Can you pray, "Our Father"?

CODE WORD: FAMILY

Today, when you talk to a family member, speak to your dad, or see a photo of him, let it be a reminder to you that you are a member of another family, a much larger one, the family of God. And remember, the true brotherhood of man is found in God's forever family, where we are more closely related to one another through the blood of Christ than to our own blood relatives who do not know Him.

CODE VERSE

As many as received Him, to them He gave the right to become children of God, to those who believe in His name. (John 1:12)

2   THE MODEL PRAYER

"Our Father in heaven, hallowed be Your name. Your
kingdom come. Your will be done on earth as it is in
heaven. Give us this day our daily bread. And forgive us
our debts, as we forgive our debtors. And do not lead us into
temptation, but deliver us from the evil one. For Yours is the
kingdom and the power and the glory forever. Amen"
—MATTHEW 6:9–13

For most of us, prayer does not come naturally, nor does it come effortlessly. It is a learned behavior. This is why the disciples requested our Lord to "teach" them to pray (Luke 11:1). In this most famous of all prayers, the Master Teacher does just that—He teaches us to pray. Even though this prayer is the most recited and repeated prayer of the Bible, Jesus never said, "Pray this prayer." In fact, earlier in this same conversation He had admonished us to "not use vain repetitions" when we pray (Matthew 6:7) but to use this prayer as a model for our praying. Thus, Jesus gives us a model, a formula, around which to construct our prayers and present our petitions before Him. His desire is that we will pray with an eye to His glory, resulting in an answer for our own good.

God is not impressed with our longwinded prayers

that are filled with lofty words and often holier-than-thou cadences in our inflective voices. He is basically saying, "Keep it simple. Pray like this from your heart."

THE OBJECT OF THIS PRAYER IS FOR GOD'S GLORY

We glorify the Lord when we are sincere in our worship, sensitive in our witness, and submissive to His will. The model prayer is 100 percent petition, and the first petition is the request that God's name be praised: "Hallowed be Your name." This involves the element of *sincere worship*. The word *hallowed* means sanctified, to be set apart. The place to begin in prayer is with an acknowledgment that the name of the Lord is different from every other name. He is holy and must be approached with reverence and respect.

God is glorified when we are not simply sincere in our worship but when we are *sensitive in our witness*. The Teacher continues admonishing us to pray, "Your kingdom come." At this point in the model prayer we are praying that the kingdom of grace might come to the hearts of those we know who need to know Jesus. But there is a larger dimension to this expression. When we request that Christ's kingdom comes, we are also praying for the coming kingdom of glory, when the Lord Jesus Christ returns to this earth and sets up His earthly kingdom, reigning and ruling from the throne of David in Jerusalem during a millennium of perfect peace.

Glorifying God in prayer also involves our being *submissive to His will*. We are to pray, "Your will be done on earth as it is in heaven." True prayer will always lead us to the place of elevating God's will over our own will in the issues of life. What Jesus preached to us on the grassy green hillside in Galilee in this model prayer, He, Himself, practiced beneath the old olive trees of Gethsemane's garden the night before He was crucified. Hear him as He prayed, "Not as I will, but as You will . . . Your will be done" (Matthew 26:39, 42). True prayer involves surrendering our own wills to His will for us.

> True prayer will always lead us to the place of elevating God's will over our own.

THE OUTCOME OF THIS PRAYER IS FOR OUR GOOD

Jesus is teaching us to ask Him for our *provision*—"Give us this day our daily bread." We are to pray with a spirit that is dependent on Him to meet our daily needs. And note, it is "daily" bread for which we are to pray. Most of us are keenly aware that the Bible relates bread to the Word of God. We need this kind of bread "daily" in our own walk with Him. What a privilege to lay our basic needs before Him and trust Him for our provision.

We are also admonished to pray not just for our provisions but for our *pardon*—"Forgive us our debts, as we forgive our debtors." True prayer will always employ this element of confession of sin in order that our sins may be forgiven. I wonder how many hundreds, perhaps thousands of times some believers have recited this prayer without ever thinking of what they are asking of the Lord. Do we truly want God to forgive us "*as*," in the same way, that we forgive those who have wronged us? This makes this a dangerous prayer to pray. Some of us are prone to say of someone who may have wronged us, "I will forgive him or her, but I won't have anything else to do with them." Is that really the way you want God to forgive you? It is a powerful thing to pray, "Forgive us our debts, as we forgive our debtors." Immediately after Jesus finishes this model prayer, the very next verse holds a powerful promise: "If you forgive men their trespasses, your heavenly Father will also forgive you" (Matthew 6:14).

Finally, Jesus teaches us to pray for *protection*—"Do not lead us into temptation, but deliver us from the evil one." Temptation is something we all face each day, and there is a vast difference in the trials we may face and the temptations that may come our way. Temptation comes from the devil to cause the believer to stumble. Trials are allowed by the Lord to enable us to stand. God will make a "way of escape" for those of us who sincerely pray for deliverance (1 Corinthians 10:13).

Jesus concludes this teaching on prayer by challenging us to pray this compelling acknowledgment that closes with a cascading crescendo: "For Yours is the kingdom and the power and the glory forever. Amen."

CODE WORD: MODEL

Today, as you go about your work and witness and see a model home or perhaps look at a set of architectural plans, let it remind you that the Lord Jesus has given you a model with which to beseech the God of heaven. Its message is plain. Its object is God's glory and its outcome is for our good!

CODE VERSE

"When you pray, go into your room . . . shut your door, pray to your Father who is in the secret place; and your Father who sees in secret will reward you openly." (Matthew 6:6)

3 GOD-HONORING PRAYER

"When you pray, you shall not be like the hypocrites. For they love to . . . be seen by men. . . . When you pray, go into your room, and when you have shut your door, pray to your Father who is in the secret place . . . And when you pray, do not use vain repetitions as the heathen do. . . . For your Father knows the things you have need of before you ask Him."
—MATTHEW 6:5–8

*I*sn't it an astounding thought that some of us are actually amazed when God answers our direct prayers? Shouldn't the opposite be true? Shouldn't we be more surprised when our prayers do not seem to have an answer? God-honoring prayers are prayed in faith and anticipating an answer.

It is of interest to note in our text that God assumes the believer is going to have a consistent prayer life. Jesus repeatedly states, "When you pray . . . When you pray . . . When you pray . . ." He does not say, "If you pray . . ." The idea that prayer is some afterthought or some emergency escape mechanism when trouble comes knocking at our door should be foreign to any believer who knows the Lord in the intimacy of Father and child. Being in constant communion with God should be like breathing; it is the natural response to our love relationship with Him.

In this introduction to the Lord's Prayer, Jesus makes mention of two types of individuals—the hypocrite and the heathen. The hypocrite, who "love[s] to pray standing in the synagogues and on the corners of the streets, that they may be seen by men," prays to impress people (Matthew 6:5). The heathen, who prays with "vain repetitions . . . for they think that they will be heard for their many words," prays in a feeble attempt to try and impress God (v. 7). If we are honest, there are times when we find a bit of the hypocrite and/ or the heathen in all of us. But the Lord says, "Do not be like them" (v. 8). God has a way of honoring sincere, secret, and simple prayers.

GOD HONORS SINCERE PRAYERS

Our Lord introduces this section of the Sermon on the Mount with a stern warning: "Take heed that you do not do your charitable deeds before men, to be seen by them. Otherwise you have no reward from your Father in heaven" (Matthew 6:1). He rebukes the hypocritical prayer life of those who "want to be seen by men." Pride and vanity are two of the greatest hindrances to God-honoring prayers. The prayers God honors are those that emerge from a sincere heart with pure motives.

Public prayers bring with them a temptation to fall into this trap. Most of us can recall hearing some who pray in public with a tone that is entirely different from their normal speech pattern. But private prayers are also susceptible to this temptation to allow pride to find its way into our prayers. For some it is difficult to fast or pray through the night without eventually telling someone about it. God invites us into His throne room of prayer, and at no time in our Christian life should we approach a matter with more sincerity of heart than when we are in sweet fellowship with Him alone. He honors sincere prayers from the heart.

GOD HONORS SECRET PRAYERS

There is something about keeping our prayer life between us and Him alone that He seems to honor. Jesus says, "When you pray, go into your room, and when you have shut your door, pray to your Father who is in the secret place; and your Father who sees in secret will reward you openly" (Matthew 6:6). Here Jesus says to keep ourselves from the temptation to be "seen by men" when we pray.

The public life of any Spirit-filled believer rests on the private life, the hidden life. There are so many object lessons revealing this truth. The beautiful high-rise office structures emerging from our city centers stand tall and firm because of their hidden life. Deep below the surface is a foundation of concrete and steel that has been dug deep into the bed-rock, enabling great buildings to glisten in the sun due to the hidden life of a solid foundation. The same is true of fruit trees from which we enjoy apples and peaches. These juicy delicacies are made possible due to the hidden life of the tree, the roots that dig deep into the earth until they find a water source through which their public life thrives. And so it is with us. God honors not only sincere prayers but secret prayers.

> The public life of any Spirit-filled believer rests on the private life, the hidden life.

GOD HONORS SIMPLE PRAYERS

Jesus admonishes us in this regard, saying, "When you pray, do not use vain repetitions as the heathen do" (Matthew 6:7). He tells us to keep it simple. After all, the Father "knows the things you have need of before you ask Him" (v. 8). It is not so much the repetition that Jesus condemns here but the "vain," meaningless repetition that often emerges from our prayers. Repetition in prayer is not vain or meaningless in many cases. Jesus Himself repeated His prayers in the garden of Gethsemane, but they were filled with sincerity and meaning.

Some of the most powerful prayers recorded in Scripture were simple prayers. Peter was sinking beneath the waves one night on the Sea of Galilee when he simply prayed, "Lord, save me!" (Matthew 14:30). And who can forget Jesus' own short, simple, but sincere prayer from the cross? "Father, forgive them, for they do not know what they do" (Luke 23:34). When you pray, remember that God is looking on your heart, and He has His ways of honoring prayers that are sincere, secret, and simple.

CODE WORD: SKYSCRAPER

Today, when you go to your office or when you pass by a tall building, let it be a reminder to you of the importance of your prayer life and how God is still in the business of honoring your prayers when they are sincere, secret, and simple.

CODE VERSE

"Your Father knows the things you have need of before you ask Him." (Matthew 6:8)

4   THE TRINITY AND PRAYER

Through Him we both have access by one Spirit to the Father.
—EPHESIANS 2:18

The holy Trinity is one of the imponderables of almighty God. God is One, manifesting Himself in three persons as the Father, the Son, and the Holy Spirit. I am not bothered by the fact that it is a great mystery and difficult to grasp. In fact, if I could understand it all, there would not be much to it. This is why the Christian life is a life of faith. Philosophy might attempt to explain it, but it cannot change. Christianity changes lives even though some of the Bible's explanations of God's grandeur and grace are unexplainable.

We often hear skeptics exclaim that the word *Trinity* cannot be found in the Bible. But we do not have to see the word to discover the truth throughout the Scripture. The Trinity—the Father, the Son, and the Holy Spirit—is present at the baptism of Jesus. The Son is standing there, the Father speaks from heaven, and the Spirit descends on the Lord like a dove from heaven (Luke 3:22).

When we come to Ephesians 2:18, we have reached one of the mountain peaks of Scripture, and the secret is found in three prepositions—*to, through,* and *by.* In this short verse is found the mystery of the Trinity in relationship to our prayer life. Prayers are to be offered "to the Father." He is the Author and Initiator of our salvation. Our prayers are to be offered "through Him [the Son]." He is the One who came to execute God's plan of redemption through His vicarious and voluntary death on the cross and His resurrection from the grave. Finally, our prayers are offered "by one Spirit." He is the One who convicts of sin, empowers us for service, and helps us in our prayer life. The Father, the Son, and the Spirit all work together in order for you and me to have access to God.

THE SOURCE OF PRAYER

Prayer is "to the Father." All true prayer begins when I claim my personal relationship with Him and begin to know and love Him in the intimacy of Father and child. For me this relationship began when I was seventeen and trusted in Christ as my personal Savior. Since that day I have grown to know Him as my heavenly Father. He is the source of our prayer life.

The only way God can be called "Father" is if we have been born again spiritually into His family through what Jesus called, in John, being born again (John 3:7). It might surprise some of us to know that we are not all God's children. We are all God's creation, but the Bible states clearly that "as many as received Him, to them He gave the right to become children of God" (John 1:12). And Paul, in his letter to the Galatians, makes it crystal clear, saying that we become children of God "through faith in Christ Jesus" (Galatians 3:26).

> The only way God can be called "Father" is if we have been born again spiritually into His family.

The gospel writers record that over seventy times Jesus began in prayer using the word *Father*. What a privilege for you and me to acknowledge that He is the source of prayer by addressing Him as Father. When we pray, we are not trying to appease a demanding parent, but we are children who, because of our relationship with Him, can come boldly before our Father's throne (Hebrews 4:16).

THE COURSE OF PRAYER

If the Father is the source of prayer, the Son is the course, through which we go to make our petitions known. Prayer is "through the Son." In fact, there is no access to the Father unless we go through the Son. The apostle Paul makes this plain: "There is one God and one Mediator between God and men, the Man Christ Jesus, who gave Himself a ransom for all" (1 Timothy 2:5–6). Apart from Christ, we have no access to God.

Jesus Christ is our High Priest. In the old dispensation on the Day of Atonement, the high priest would take the blood of a sacrificial lamb, enter beyond the veil of the Holy of Holies, and sprinkle the blood on the mercy seat of the ark. Jesus Christ, the Lamb of God, made the final sacrifice for sin. He shed His blood on the cross, died, and rose the third day, passed through the heavens, and presented His own blood at the throne of God. No wonder Paul said, "Through Him we both have access by one Spirit to the Father."

It is through Christ—not through the church, not through a priest, not through the Virgin Mary, but through Him and Him alone. Jesus is the course of true prayer.

THE FORCE OF PRAYER

Effective, powerful prayer is "by one Spirit." If the Father is the source and the Son is the course, then the Spirit is the force behind it all. It is the Holy Spirit praying in us and through us that empowers us to pray with results. Jude reminds us that we are built up in our most holy faith when we are "praying in the Holy Spirit" (Jude v. 20).

It is the Holy Spirit who "helps in our weaknesses. For we do not know what we should pray for as we ought" (Romans 8:26). We can read the great prayers of saints down through the ages. We can recite prayers by rote from memory. But without the Holy Spirit we will never be effective in our prayer journey. It is only through Christ and "by one Spirit" that we can touch the Father in prayer.

Access to the Father is the goal of all prayer. He is the source. We must go through His Son and be empowered by His Spirit. Yes, "For *through Him* [Jesus] we both have access *by one Spirit to the Father.*"

CODE WORD: ICE

Today, when you see a piece of ice in your glass, let it be a reminder that H_2O is found in three forms: liquid, solid, or steam. Three manifestations of the same H_2O. And so the holy Trinity manifests Himself in three persons: the Father, who is the source of our prayer; the Son, who is the course of our prayer; and the Spirit, who is the force behind it all.

CODE VERSE

There is one God and one Mediator between God and men, the Man Christ Jesus, who gave Himself a ransom for all. (1 Timothy 2:5–6)

5   PRAYER ACCORDING TO THE WILL OF GOD

"Ask, and it will be given to you; seek, and you will
find; knock, and it will be opened to you."
—MATTHEW 7:7

The prayer that gets results is the prayer that is prayed in accordance with the will of God in a matter. The apostle John reminds us that we can have confidence in the Lord and that "if we ask anything *according to His will*, He hears us. And if we know that He hears us, whatever we ask, we know that we have the petitions that we have asked of Him" (1 John 5:14–15, emphasis added).

On a grassy green hillside in Galilee, our Lord taught us the three levels of prayer that accompany all growing believers. And each of these levels is directly related to the will of God for our lives. First, He instructs us to "ask." When we know the will of God for a circumstance or situation, we are to simply ask and "it will be given to you." If we do not know the will of God for a specific matter for which we are praying, we are to "seek" His will. And when we do, He promises we "will find" it. Finally, if we are certain of God's will in a matter but have yet to see the answer, Jesus summons us to "knock," to keep on knocking, and "it will be opened" to us.

THE LEVEL OF PRESENTING A PETITION

We begin with the level of *presenting a petition*. We are to "ask." This sounds so simple, but it is a difficult beginning for some people. There are those who are so proud and so self-sufficient that they seldom ask anyone for anything. Thus, the thought of asking God for something does not come easy.

Ask . . . this little three-letter, one-syllable word is one of the most important words in life. Those in sales are not successful until they ask for the sale. Few politicians would be elected unless they make the ask for people's votes and support. Medical doctors would have difficulty in their diagnosis without asking the patient a series of questions. Most of what we have learned in life is because we have learned to ask questions.

Jesus was keenly aware of this fact; thus He reveals that the first level of prayer is simply to "ask." And when this is done "according to His will," He promises that our petitions will "be given" to us. This does not mean that whatever we ask for we will receive. There are times we ask God for things that are not in our best interest. Any of us who have raised children have, at times, denied things for which they have asked because we knew what was best for them at the time. Quite honestly, I am thankful that God has not granted everything I have asked Him across the years. There have been times that I have sincerely asked Him something that, in the moment, I deeply desired. But in retrospect, I realize He denied it because He had something far better for me.

When we pray on the level of presenting a petition, the key is knowing and having assurance of the will of God in a matter. And, when we do, we "ask and it will be given" to us.

THE LEVEL OF PRESSING A PETITION

The next level of prayer is the level of *pressing a petition*. Jesus says, "Seek and you will find." This is the prayer we pray when we do not know the will of God in a particular matter. We seek until we find it. This is the prayer for knowledge of the revealed will of God in a matter.

This prayer is a deeper level of praying. It goes a step further than asking. This prayer demands the sacrifice of an intense search for the heart of God. Many believers never progress past the level of simply presenting a petition to the level of pressing a petition in search of God's will. This is the prayer that is coupled with the Word of God in order to find the will of God. As Paul said, "Let the word of Christ dwell in you richly in all wisdom" (Colossians 3:16). Keep seeking, and stand on His promise, and you will find!

THE LEVEL OF PERSISTING IN A PETITION

The higher level of prayer is the one of *persisting in a petition*. "Knock, and it will be opened to you." Knocking implies perseverance such as we see in Jesus' story of the man who came to his friend's home at midnight and continued knocking on his door until the friend opened it (Luke 11:5–8).

This is the prayer we pray when we are confident of God's will in a matter but have not yet seen the answer. We persist in prayer. The verb tense indicates that this is continuous action. We are to keep on knocking.

> "Knock, and it will be opened to you."
>
> MATTHEW 7:7

Those of us who have raised children know that when they are small, we teach them to "ask." As they grow, we teach them to "seek" for their desires. And because we know what is best for them, we teach them to show real earnestness until doors are open for them. Problems arise in some homes because parents never allow their children to get past level one. They are given everything for which they ask and are never taught to seek . . . much less knock.

The three levels of prayer are prayed in relationship to the will of God for our lives. If you know God's will in a matter, "ask and you will receive." If you don't know God's will, "seek and you will find" it. If you are confident of the will of God in the matter for which you are praying but have not yet seen the answer, don't give up; keep on knocking "and it will be opened to you."

CODE WORD: DOOR

Today, when you come to a closed door, let it be a reminder to you of the importance of not just presenting a petition to God, but of moving on to pressing your petition and beyond that to persisting with it. You have the promises of God on your side; you will receive, you will find, it will be opened to you.

CODE VERSE

If we ask anything according to His will, He hears us. And if we know that He hears us, whatever we ask, we know that we have the petitions that we have asked of Him. (1 John 5:14–15)

6   OUR PRAYER PARTNER

The Spirit also helps in our weaknesses. For we do not know what
we should pray for as we ought, but the Spirit Himself makes
intercession for us with groanings which cannot be uttered. Now He
who searches the hearts knows what the mind of the Spirit is, because
He makes intercession for the saints according to the will of God.
—ROMANS 8:26–27

*H*ave you ever had a prayer partner, one who shared your prayer needs, one with whom you agreed on a matter, one who believed with you for the answer to your deepest prayer need? Well, there is good news for you. You have such a person, and He is with you all the time, searching the innermost recesses of your heart, helping you in your weakness, making intercession for you, and always doing so according to the Lord's will. His sweet name is the Holy Spirit, and He lives in the life of every believer.

The Bible teaches that your body is "the temple of the Holy Spirit" (1 Corinthians 6:19). The Greek word translated "temple" in this verse means the inner sanctum, the Holy of Holies. Your very body is the Holy Spirit's "holy place." Think on that just a moment. The Holy Spirit, who is in you, kneels at the altar of your heart. You are His place of worship. He does in your body what the Son does before the Father, making intercession. The Holy Spirit is our personal prayer partner, and we can learn more about Him and His ministry in us by asking several pertinent questions.

> The Holy Spirit is our personal prayer partner.

A *WHAT* QUESTION

What does the Spirit actually do? He "helps" us to pray (Romans 8:26). This word literally means to lend a hand. This word is used only one other time in the entire New Testament. It is found in Bethany when Martha requested of the Lord that her sister, Mary, "help" her in the kitchen (Luke 10:40). This is what the Spirit does for us. He lends a hand. He comes alongside us and takes part in our prayers with us, making our prayer life more effective and efficient.

The truth is we are weak, and we need help, especially when it comes to praying. We don't find this kind of help in books or prayer journals. We have a prayer partner . . . in us . . . right now . . . and just like someone who picks up a dish towel and helps us with the dishes, the Spirit "helps" us in our prayer life.

A *WHERE* QUESTION

Where does the Holy Spirit help us? He helps in our "weakness." This word is at times translated "crippled" or "invalid" in Scripture. The truth is many of us are not very healthy when it comes to having an effective prayer life. Jesus knew this. After all, His own disciples could not even watch and pray with Him for an hour in His greatest time of need. So He sent each believer a prayer partner, the Holy Spirit, to help us where we are weak.

However, just because someone is there to help us does not mean we let them. Some of us are too proud to admit we are weak, much less in need of help. Unfortunately, some "resist the Holy Spirit" (Acts 7:51), others "grieve the Holy Spirit" (Ephesians 4:30) by never acknowledging their need of His help, and some "quench the Spirit" (1 Thessalonians 5:19) when they continue to live with unconfessed sin.

What does the Holy Spirit do for us? He helps us. And where does He help us? In our weaknesses. This brings us to the next question: Why?

A *WHY* QUESTION

Why does the Spirit help us in our weaknesses? Because "we do not know what we should pray for as we ought." The Greek word translated "ought" appears over one hundred times in the New Testament, and the majority of those times it is translated "must." An example is in the well-known passage in John 3:7, "You must be born again." God brings His plans into being through the prayers of His people. Therefore, we must pray. It is not just that you and I ought to pray; we must pray!

It is so apparently true that we do not always know how we ought to pray. Even Paul prayed three times in 2 Corinthians 12 for his "thorn in the flesh" to be removed. The truth is we often do not know how to pray as we ought because we cannot see into the future. We need help. We are weak. Like our own children, we often have a difficult time confusing our needs with our wants and do not know for sure what is really best for us.

In the language of the New Testament, there is a definite article before "what" here in Romans 8:26 as if to convey that we do not know "the what" for which to pray. This is not just general saying of our prayers here but a very specific need for which we need help in praying. We have a prayer partner who helps us in our weaknesses because we do not know "the what" for which to pray as we ought.

A *HOW* QUESTION

Finally, how does the Holy Spirit help us pray? He "makes intercession" for us. That is, He pleads on our behalf before the Father's throne. This thought is closely akin to the good Samaritan, who happened upon a beaten man in trouble by the highway side. He got involved, interceded on the man's behalf, took him to an inn, paid his bill, and met his needs

(Luke 10:25–37). This is how the Holy Spirit moves in our prayer lives. We are weak. We do not know how to pray as we ought. So, He comes alongside to help us, pleading on our behalf.

The key in understanding how the Spirit "helps" us is that He knows the mind of God and always prays "according to the will of God" (Romans 8:27). He leads us to the will of God for our lives. And we can find God's will through the Scripture and through the Spirit. There are many things we know for certain are God's will because they are plainly stated in the Bible. But in other matters we may not be certain. At this point the Spirit helps us "because He makes intercession for the saints according to the will of God."

This is why the Bible is called the "sword of the Spirit" (Ephesians 6:17). We need both. Some have the Bible but are unaware of the Spirit. Others have the Spirit but are without the Scriptures. To find God's will, we trust in His revealed Word to us as we yield to the Holy Spirit because He intercedes for us always according to the will of God.

CODE WORD: KITCHEN

Today, when you walk into your kitchen to prepare a meal or to wash the dishes, remember that just as Martha needed Mary's practical help in the kitchen, so the Holy Spirit is in you to help you in your weaknesses because you don't know how to pray as you ought in a given matter.

CODE VERSE

Do you not know that your body is the temple of the Holy Spirit who is in you, whom you have from God, and you are not your own? (1 Corinthians 6:19)

7 A TALE OF TWO PRAYERS

"Two men went up to the temple to pray, one a Pharisee and the other
a tax collector. The Pharisee stood and prayed thus with himself,
'God, I thank You that I am not like other men—extortioners, unjust,
adulterers, or even as this tax collector. I fast twice a week; I give tithes
of all that I possess.' And the tax collector, standing afar off, would
not so much as raise his eyes to heaven, but beat his breast, saying,
'God, be merciful to me a sinner!' I tell you, this man went down
to his house justified rather than the other; for everyone who exalts
himself will be humbled, and he who humbles himself will be exalted."
—LUKE 18:10–14

*W*ise teachers are those who seek to show their students a
deep truth rather than merely telling them some truth.
Jesus was the master storyteller. So many of His most often
repeated lessons were those He told in parables, stories that
painted deeper meanings in their telling. In the parable of
the Pharisee and the publican, He taught some of His most
pointed and poignant prayer principles by contrasting two
people, two prayers, and two paradoxes.

JESUS EVALUATES TWO PEOPLE
One of those mentioned who went to pray was a Pharisee.
The Pharisees were the strict and rigid formalists of their

day. They were known for the way they often called attention to themselves by pulling their ecclesiastical garments snugly around themselves as they walked through the crowds. Many people mentioned in the New Testament, such as Nicodemus and Paul, had roots in pharisaical thought.

The Pharisee was joined by a publican, a tax collector. The tax collector of the first-century world in Jerusalem was among the most despised of all people. He was a Jew who took up Roman taxes from his own people. Corruption and overcharging of taxes went hand in hand with his job. We'll never know how many people this particular publican in our parable had cheated. How many times he had taken the only cow of someone behind on their taxes or removed the furniture from the home of some needy widow is forever unknown.

Jesus begins by contrasting these two people who went to pray: one was revered by man, and the other was reviled by most of first-century Jewish Jerusalem.

JESUS EXAMINES TWO PRAYERS

Jesus begins by stating the Pharisee "stood" out where he could be readily seen. I envision him with outstretched arms as he shouted his prayer. Note Jesus observed he prayed "with himself." Most of us have heard prayers of this sort when we got the feeling that the intercessor was not talking to God but informing himself and others of his own greatness. There are five instances of the use of the perpendicular pronoun, *I*, found in this two-sentence petition. "I thank you . . . I am not like other men . . . I fast twice a week . . . I give tithes . . . of all that I possess." Pharisees always measure themselves on a human standard "as other men" as opposed to God's standard of Christ's perfect righteousness. This man didn't go to the temple to pray; he went to inform God and others of how wonderful he was.

> This man didn't go to the temple to pray; he went to inform God and others of how wonderful he was.

Contrast this prayer with that of the tax collector. He "stood afar off" and deemed himself so unworthy he could "not so much as raise his eyes to heaven." In a moment of deep remorse and repentance, he "beat his breast" and pleaded, "God, be merciful to me a sinner."

The message is plain. God looks on the heart. Those filled with self-pride are simply blinded to spiritual reality. It is more important who we are when we pray and how we pray than what we say with the words that issue from our mouths.

JESUS EXPLAINS TWO PARADOXES

As for the Pharisee, our Lord says, "Everyone who exalts himself will be humbled." That is, the way down is up! Those like the Pharisee soon learn that they should have been seeking the applause of God rather than the applause of men. God has His own ways of humbling those whose pride rules their lives.

As for the publican, our Lord says, "He who humbles himself will be exalted." That is, the way up is down! In humility the tax collector sought only the applause of God as he prayed, and Jesus said, "I tell you, this man went down to his house justified rather than the other."

Luke records this parable of Jesus for all posterity. It is a lesson each of us needs to read and heed. It is a tale of two people. Maybe, like the tax collector, you have made some mistakes in life for which you are truly sorry. One failure doesn't make a flop. You can bat again. It is a tale of two prayers. When you pray, remember that attitude and humility go a long way in pleasing God. And it is a tale of two paradoxes. It is a truth of the ages that "everyone who exalts himself will be humbled." Everyone. And, "He who humbles himself will be exalted." Make this tax collector your prayer partner and you, too, will go down to your house justified.

CODE WORD: TAXES

The next time you work on your income taxes or note the amount of taxes deducted from your pay stub, let it remind you of this parable of Jesus. Make this tax man's prayer a model for your own, and, always remember, the way up is down!

CODE VERSE

"Whoever exalts himself will be humbled, and he who humbles himself will be exalted." (Luke 14:11)

8   A PRAYER FOR A NEW BEGINNING

Have mercy upon me, O God . . . blot out my transgressions . . .
wash me . . . cleanse me . . . . I acknowledge my transgressions,
and my sin is always before me. Against You, and You only,
have I sinned . . . Purge me. . . . wash me . . . Create in me a
clean heart . . . Restore to me the joy of Your salvation.
—PSALM 51:1–12

One is prone to wonder how King David, in light of such failings in life, not the least of which was his notorious adulterous affair with Bathsheba, could end up being such a spiritual giant, producing inspiring and God-honoring psalms. But in reading his prayer of repentance in Psalm 51, all wonder soon vanishes. In these words he laid bare his heart to God, and to us. He was sin sick. He realized that sin is at the very heart of so many wrecked and ruined lives, and he learned how to deal with it and put it away.

Psalm 51 is a paradigm for the type of prayer that leads to forgiveness—one that issues out of true repentance. Repentance is not simply remorse, being sorry for our sin. The rich young ruler in Luke 18:18–23 went away sorrowful but didn't repent. It is not simply regret. Pilate regretted his deed, as we see in Matthew 27:24, but there is no evidence he repented. It is not reform, turning over a new leaf. Judas reformed. He took the thirty pieces of silver back to the priests from which they'd come, but he did not repent (Matthew 26:14–16). Repentance is a true change of mind, which results in a change of volition, which then results in a change of action. Nowhere is it pictured in any more graphic and instructive detail than here in this prayer of David.

This psalm has comforted believers through the centuries with the fact that if King David could find forgiveness and a new beginning, so can we. This can happen when we, like David, take these three important steps: assume responsibility, seek reconciliation, and embrace the restoration process.

ASSUME PERSONAL RESPONSIBILITY

In the first six verses of Psalm 51 we find David taking *personal responsibility*. Some never find a place of new beginnings because they refuse to take personal responsibility for their sin. In their minds their failures are always someone else's fault. Listen to David as he appeals for mercy. He knew he was responsible for his sin and undeserving of God's grace and forgiveness, so he made his appeal on the basis of God's mercy. He took responsibility. Note the intensely personal pronouns in this prayer: "My transgressions . . . my sin . . . my iniquity."

David realized that sin hounds us. He acknowledged, "My sin is always before me." Everywhere he turned he saw the ghost of his guilty and wicked past. When he passed a cemetery, he saw the tomb of Uriah, Bathsheba's husband. Every morning he witnessed it in the wounded eyes of Bathsheba and in the cynical stares of Joab, his trusted confidant and military leader. The servants knew. Everyone knew. It was always before him.

He also was keenly aware of how sin will not simply hound us but haunt us as well. Listen to him: "Against You, You only, have I sinned." The most haunting thing about his transgressions was that they were not just against Uriah, or Bathsheba, or their baby who died so young; his sins were primarily against God. So he unloaded his confession before God, never once offering any self-justification for his wrongs. He pleaded for forgiveness. He modeled for each of us coming after him the road back to God. It begins when we, like the king, take personal responsibility for our own sin.

> Sin will not simply hound us but haunt us as well.

SEEK RECONCILIATION

Next, he saw the need of *private reconciliation* with God Himself. He pleaded with the Lord, "Purge me . . . wash me . . . Hide Your face from my sins, and blot out all my iniquities. Create in me a clean heart . . . Restore to me the joy of Your salvation" (Psalm 51:7–12). When David asked God to "create" in him a brand-new heart, he used the same word used in the first chapter of the Bible that explains the creative activity of God, who can make something out of nothing. We can never do this for ourselves, no matter how hard we may try. This is something private between us and God. Reconciliation is the response of a loving God to the true repentance of His people. David longed to see the joy of the salvation he'd once known restored afresh and anew.

EMBRACE THE RESTORATION PROCESS

The process of personal recognition and private reconciliation led David to a *public restoration*. The newly pardoned king began to plead on behalf of others. He continued his prayer, promising to "teach transgressors Your ways, and sinners shall be converted to You" (v. 13). Once forgiven, David burst forth in praise to God, saying, "O Lord, open my lips, and my mouth shall show forth Your praise" (v. 15). For months his lips had been sealed in shame, refusing to admit or acknowledge his wrongs. But like anyone and everyone who has tasted God's forgiveness of their own sin, when David's sin was confessed and forsaken, his first impulse was to not hold back his praise in the direction of his loving and merciful Lord.

There is a valuable life lesson here for each of us. Everything we cover, God will uncover. Sin will hound you and haunt you and eventually be revealed for all to see. But there is a flip side. And it is good news. David learned that everything we uncover, God will cover . . . and lead us with a new heart to our own new beginning.

CODE WORD: BEDCOVERS

Tonight, when you pull the covers up over your body when going to sleep, let it be a reminder to you that the more you try to cover your own sin, the more it will eventually be uncovered. But when you uncover it before God, He will cover it in forgiveness before the world around you. And that, friend, is good news.

CODE VERSE

He who covers his sins will not prosper, but whoever confesses and forsakes them will have mercy. (Proverbs 28:13)

9   TRUE CONFESSION

If we confess our sins, He is faithful and just to forgive us
our sins and to cleanse us from all unrighteousness.

—1 JOHN 1:9

*T*he Lord deals with our sin at the moment of conversion through His finished work on the cross. This is why we read in 1 John 1:7, "The blood of Jesus Christ His Son cleanses us from all sin." Note "sin" is singular, indicating our inherent sin nature. But what about our "sins"? Just because we trust in Christ does not mean we will no longer commit acts of transgressions, sins (plural). These are to be dealt with through continual confession—"If we confess our sins, He is faithful and just to forgive us our sins."

Perhaps no other word in our Christian vocabulary is as misunderstood and misapplied as the word *confession*. Some seem to think it is remorse—that is, feeling sorry about our sin. Others confuse confession with regret, simply regretting some sinful act. Still others confuse confession with reform, that is, trying to turn over a new leaf and starting again. The only way to find God's forgiveness is through true confession. Thus the apostle John in this chapter points to three important steps to find God's forgiveness. He argues that forgiveness is conditional, confessional, and continual.

FORGIVENESS IS CONDITIONAL

Forgiveness is conditioned on a big *if*. "*If* we confess our sins, He is faithful and just to forgive our sins." So many of God's promises in the Bible are conditioned on our actions, and in some cases our reactions. Take the often repeated promise in 2 Chronicles 7:14: "*If* My people who are called by My name will humble themselves, and pray and seek My face, and turn from their wicked ways, *then* I will hear from heaven, and will forgive their sin and heal their land" (emphasis added).

Many of us have lived our entire lives prefaced with an *if*. *If only I had had more time. If only I had not made that bad decision. If only . . .* As I mentioned above, being forgiven of our sins hinges on a big *if*: *if* we confess our sins, He is faithful to forgive. Forgiveness is conditional on our confession of sin. Without it there is no forgiveness.

FORGIVENESS IS CONFESSIONAL

Confession does not simply mean that we admit what we have done and are sorry for it. The word *confess* in 1 John 1:9 translates a compound word in Greek literally meaning "to say the same as God says" or more simply stated "to agree with God." When I confess my sins, I am agreeing with God about it being so serious that it necessitated the cross. It is not some little vice I can excuse by claiming everyone else is doing it. We have all sorts of ways of avoiding confession.

We say it is not anger; it is righteous indignation. We insist it is not lust, simply an appealing glance. But true confession agrees with God and calls sin what it is: sin.

> When I confess my sins, I am agreeing with God about it being so serious that it necessitated the cross.

Any of us who have raised children have seen this played out. We are all sitting at the breakfast table and someone knocks over the milk. Everyone scurries to stand up and blot it out with their napkins . . . except the culprit, who often asks, "What happened?" Or, someone cheats on a business deal and God asks, "What happened?" The quick answer is that it was the pressure of the economy, followed by other excuses. Confession agrees with the God of truth. Confession says, "I knocked over the milk" . . . "I cheated on the deal."

The good news is that the Lord Jesus is ready and willing to forgive any and all our sins, old habit patterns, tangled relationships, or whatever ensnares us . . . *if* we remember that forgiveness is conditional on our true confession, which is agreement with God.

FORGIVENESS IS CONTINUAL

There is a distinction between the root (our sin) and the fruit (our sins). Our sin (singular) nature is dealt with on the cross (1 John 1:7). When you were converted to Christ, you didn't have to confess all your "sins" simply to be saved. Who among us could even begin to remember the majority of them?

While our "sin" is dealt with at the cross, our "sins" should be dealt with in continual confession according to 1 John 1:9. Confession of our sins should be continual not in order to be saved but to be in fellowship with the Father. Believers can never do anything to break their relationship with Christ, but unconfessed sins can cloud our fellowship with Him. The verb in 1 John 1:9 expresses continuous action. That is, we must keep on confessing our sins. This should be the constant attitude of the believer.

What happens when we confess our sins to God? In a court of law, when a guilty person confesses, they are condemned and sentenced. But with God when we confess our sins to Him, we find complete and total forgiveness. How is this possible? Your sin has already been punished in the body of Christ on the cross, and, based on the Lord's own character, "He is faithful and just" to forgive you. Yes, God is not only faithful; He is a just God. For Him to free you of your own sin, He had to condemn His own Son and cause Him to take your sins in His own body on the cross and suffer God's punishment for you there.

When our daughter was young, she took piano lessons. She would practice a new piece, make it through the first couple of lines of music, and make a mistake. Then start all over . . . until she got to the same place and made the same mistake. Then start over again . . . and again. Some of us have tried to start over in life so many times. We don't need a new and louder beginning. We already know those first bars of the Christian life by heart. We need to keep going, confess our sins when we make a mistake, and finish the song.

CODE WORD: MUSIC

Today, when you hear a song on the radio, let it remind you that your life may hit some bumps, you may make some mistakes, but confession is what keeps us moving forward to the completion of our own song.

CODE VERSE

I acknowledged my sin to You, and my iniquity I have not hidden. I said, "I will confess my transgressions to the LORD," and You forgave the iniquity of my sin. Selah. (Psalm 32:5)

10   PRAYER AND REVIVAL

"If My people who are called by My name will humble
themselves, and pray and seek My face, and turn
from their wicked ways, then I will hear from heaven,
and will forgive their sin and heal their land."
—2 CHRONICLES 7:14

*R*ecently while passing through the kitchen, where my wife was preparing the evening meal, my eyes fell on an old note card that had yellowed through the decades. Looking closely I noted my mother's handwriting on it. It was her old recipe for one of my favorite childhood dishes. When prepared precisely as my mom had directed, it tasted exactly like the dish she used to make.

Within the heart of each of us is a longing for something more, a new season of refreshing, a revival. Did you know that God has His own recipe for revival in our hearts? He has even written it down for all of us to follow: "If My people will . . . pray . . . then I will hear from heaven." When this recipe is followed precisely and put into practice, it will enable us to soar into regions of spiritual reanimation some of us have never known. God's recipe employs four distinct steps.

GOD'S DESIRE

"If My people . . . then . . ." God is waiting, willing, even long-ing to send a new spirit of revival to His people. However, while in the purest sense revival is always a sovereign work of almighty God, like any recipe it has some conditions attached to it. It is conditional. The Bible says, "If *My* people . . ." Revival begins with us, those who are born into His family, and not with the lost world around us. If certain conditions are met, certain results are sure to follow.

There is a very real sense in which personal revival is not a miracle dropping out of the sky on us. It is simply God's promised response to conditions met by His own people. God's desire is to send a fresh wind of His Spirit on me . . . and you.

GOD'S DESIGN

Personal revival is conditional on God's own people. This is a family matter. He is addressing "My people" here. It begins with you and me. Read the history of any of the great spiri-tual awakenings that shook regions and cultures of the world and you will find that they usually began when one man, or one woman, came under deep conviction and became des-perate to be anointed with what the psalmist called "fresh oil" (Psalm 92:10).

God's real problem today is not with a culture that has

gone awry but with His own people called by His own name. While many point to the decay of our culture resulting in a decline in the moral fabric and the godless factors surrounding so much in politics, God reveals that the real issue is not with "them" but with "us." Or, as Jesus put it, we should stop trying to get a small splinter out of someone else's eye while there is a large beam sticking out of ours (Matthew 7:3–5). God's design for revival begins with you and me, and all God's people.

GOD'S DEMAND

God's demand begins first with a call for His own people to "humble themselves" by recognizing and confessing their need to seek Him in all things. We must be on constant vigil to guard against a spiritual pride that results in self-centeredness. True humility involves a broken spirit before the Lord.

> True humility involves a broken spirit before the Lord.

Second, we are to pray. This is not a call to a mere recitation of prayers but an earnest calling out to Him. Prayer is warfare. Too many believers' prayer lives can be summed up in the first four words of Ephesians 6:12: "For we wrestle not" (KJV). Every true revival in history has been born and cradled in the place of prayer. It is recorded of the early church that "when they had prayed, the place where they were assembled together was shaken; and they were all filled with the Holy Spirit, and they spoke the word of God with boldness" (Acts 4:31).

Next, God demands that we "seek [His] face." If we spent as much time in our prayers seeking His face as we do His hand to help us, we would be much nearer to personal revival. And that is not all. He demands we "turn from [our] wicked ways." Sin that is unconfessed and therefore unforgiven is the greatest obstacle to revival. Solomon, who knew this from personal experience, reminds us, "He who covers his sins will not prosper, but whoever confesses and forsakes them will have mercy" (Proverbs 28:13). It is not simply enough to be sorry over our sins or to even confess them. We must forsake them in true repentance.

GOD'S DELIGHT

God delights in forgiving our sin. He promises to "hear from heaven . . . forgive our sin . . . and heal our land." In fact, God delights more in healing our hearts and our homes than we do ourselves, for it appropriates His sacrifice on the cross and does not render His death in vain in our concerns. He is willing, waiting, and longing to be faithful to His promise when we come to Him on His conditions.

If my own daughter and I had a misunderstanding or she had done something to break our fellowship, my heart would long for restoration. If she came to me in brokenness and humility, asked for forgiveness, and looked lovingly into my face, how do you think I would respond? Of course, I would forgive and welcome her into my open arms with an open heart. How much more will your heavenly Father respond to you in such a way?

God has a recipe for revival. "If My people . . . then will I hear from heaven." Our part is not that difficult. Just follow the directions.

CODE WORD: DINNER

Tonight, when you sit down to eat your dinner, let it remind you that the one who prepared it followed a certain recipe. There is a recipe for personal revival—humble yourself, pray, seek His face, turn from your sinful ways. And He will hear from heaven and receive you with open arms.

CODE VERSE

Will You not revive us again, that Your people may rejoice in You? (Psalm 85:6)

11 MAKING THE ASK

At Gibeon the Lord appeared to Solomon in a dream by
night; and God said, "Ask! What shall I give you?"
—1 KINGS 3:5

*D*uring my high school days, I had a weekend sales job at a shoe store. I will never forget the instruction I received from the manager on my first day. He said, above all, when you let a customer try on the shoe and tell them about its features, do not forget to ask for the sale. Making the ask is what separates successful salespeople from others. The same holds true with those of us who are tasked with raising money for worthy causes. There comes a time when you must make the ask.

Young Solomon was about to be crowned king of his father, David's, impressive and massive empire. He was not yet twenty years of age and would be following in the footsteps of one of the greatest leaders and motivators of men in human history. At this time in his life, his heart was pure and virtually empty of pride. He journeyed to Gibeon for the express purpose of seeking God's direction. And God met him with this admonition—"Ask! What shall I give you?"

What do you want? What you want may not be what you need, but it is often a good indication of where your heart is.

And herein lies a greater danger than not getting what you want. It is wanting something, getting it, and then realizing it is not what you needed after all.

Solomon had the right answer. He had his priorities in the right order. He didn't have to think long and hard for an answer. Right away he replied, "Give to Your servant an understanding heart to judge Your people, that I may discern between good and evil" (1 Kings 3:9). Solomon asked for three things. He wanted God to work with him, not with others; to work in him, not around him; and to work through him, not for him.

Ask! How many dozens of times in the Gospels do we hear this word escape the lips of our Lord as He addresses us? On virtually every page is an invitation from Him to ask Him to meet our needs. This simple word is a key to prayer. It is a tragedy that so many are too proud to ask for anything.

WHEN YOU PRAY, ASK GOD TO WORK *WITH* YOU

Solomon asked that God would work with him, not just with someone else. He knew that his greatest need began in his own heart and not in someone else's.

For some of us the problems we encounter are always someone else's fault in our minds. Wives blame husbands, kids blame parents, and we sometimes blame God. Had

> What is it that you really want from God?

the old spiritual already been written, Solomon would be singing, "It's not my brother, not my sister, but it's me, oh Lord, standing in the need of prayer."

Ask. What is it that you really want from God? Start by asking God to work with you . . . not always with someone else. Solomon said essentially, "Lord, I want to be right with You. I want You to work with me first and foremost."

WHEN YOU PRAY, ASK GOD TO WORK *IN* YOU

Solomon knew his greatest need was internal, not external. He asked God for "an understanding heart." Too often we go about trying to change the world with external forces. We are prone to think social activism, shouting a little louder, or beating our Bibles a bit more forcefully will effect change, when what we really need is an internal change of heart.

Solomon asked for something inside him that he did not have—wisdom. He had the greatest education money could buy, but he recognized there was a difference between knowledge and wisdom. Knowledge is the accumulation of facts; wisdom is the ability to take those facts, discern them, and then make the right decisions from them.

One of our greatest needs is "an understanding heart."

Solomon could have asked for anything. But he knew his greatest need was for God to work in him and not just outside him. After all, if we have a heart that can hear from God, understanding His will and way for us, what else would we ever need to live life well? Ask God to work in you, not just outside of you.

WHEN YOU PRAY, ASK GOD TO WORK *THROUGH* YOU

Too often we think our need is to ask God to work for us, to bless us, instead of asking Him to work through us to be a blessing to others. Solomon asked God to work through him.

God may be asking you, right now, "What do you want?" Are most of your requests designed primarily to benefit you or to bless others? Think about it. Solomon chose the best, and God threw in the rest. The Lord said, "I have done according to your words; see, I have given you a wise and understanding heart . . . And I have also given you what you have not asked: both riches and honor, so that there shall not be anyone like you among the kings all your days" (vv. 12–13).

However, there is a sad postscript. When your blessings start to be held closer than the Blesser, you can cease hearing from God. Solomon, blessed with great power and wisdom, allowed his focus to begin to shift. Slowly at first, but when he was an old man he concluded that "Vanity of vanities . . . All is vanity" (Ecclesiastes 12:8). In Ecclesiastes we hear from an old man whose heart can no longer hear from God. But in the end, listen to the hard-won wisdom of Solomon's last words—"Remember now your Creator in the days of your youth . . . Hear the conclusion of the whole matter: Fear God and keep His commandments, for this is man's all" (Ecclesiastes 12:1, 13).

What do you want? Ask. The good news is when you choose the best, God will more than bless.

CODE WORD: ASK

Today, every time someone asks you a question or you ask someone for something, let it be a reminder to you that God invites you to come before Him with boldness and make the ask. Ask Him to work with you, in you, and through you.

CODE VERSE

"Ask of Me, and I will give You the nations for Your inheritance, and the ends of the earth for Your possession." (Psalm 2:8)

12   THE PRAYER OF JABEZ

Jabez called on the God of Israel saying, "Oh, that You would
bless me indeed, and enlarge my territory, that Your hand would
be with me, and that You would keep me from evil, that I may
not cause pain!" So God granted him what he requested.
—1 CHRONICLES 4:10

*J*abez is a man almost no one knows. He is tucked away
in the maze of five hundred different names listed in
the beginning chapters of 1 Chronicles. Most of these names
are obscure and even unpronounceable, and never heard
again. Hardly anyone knew Jabez then, and fewer know him
now. Type his name and spell check immediately changes the
spelling to "James." His biography occupies only a couple of
dozen words in all the Bible. He is introduced in one verse
and then rather abruptly dismissed in the next. And that is
it. He is never mentioned again.

But Jabez prayed one of the most poignant and productive prayers in all the Bible. The Bible says he was "more
honorable than his brothers" (1 Chronicles 4:9). Jabez was
not one of the boys. He never flocked like the geese in forma-
tion; he soared like an eagle above them all. He was proactive,
wanting to experience all God had for him. Thus, he left us
a prayer that each of us should make our own. He prayed for

productivity: "Bless me . . . enlarge my territory." He prayed for power: ". . . that your hand would be with me." And he prayed for purity: "Keep me from evil." What a difference this prayer can make when we incorporate its truth into our daily prayers.

JABEZ TEACHES US TO *PRAY FOR PRODUCTIVITY*

Hear his plea, "Oh, that You would bless me indeed, and enlarge my territory." He is pleading with God for more opportunity, more responsibility, more influence. A person's "territory" has to do with their sphere of influence. Paul reminded us that there is an "area of influence God assigned to us" (2 Corinthians 10:13 ESV).

Jabez focused in a forward direction. He was not content with the status quo or some form of spiritual mediocrity. He was praying with a spirit of conquest, not content with who he was but focused on who he could become. Take this personal petition with you today. Ask God to increase your influence in every sphere of life, to "enlarge your territory."

JABEZ TEACHES US TO *PRAY FOR POWER*

He continues pleading that God's own hand be on him and with him: "Bless me . . . enlarge my territory . . . that Your hand would be with me." In the Bible God's hand is always a symbol of His power. Jabez was wise enough to know that if God blessed him and gave him expanded influence, he could not go forward in his own strength alone; he needed God's own hand to rest on him with power.

I once asked a medical student the most intriguing aspect of dissecting the cadaver, which is required in the first year of medical studies. Without hesitation, the aspiring young physician said, "Dissecting the man's hands." The hand is such an amazing appendage. So many expressions emerge from it—pointed fingers of accusation, clenched fists of anger, hands clasped in prayer, or outstretched in welcome. I think of what my own hands have done for my daughters. They held them as babies, carried them when they could not walk, lifted them up when they fell, wiped their tears when they were hurting, disciplined them when needed, gave them thousands of pats on the back, clapped for them at concerts and games too numerous to mention, and pointed the way for them through the intersections of life. My girls want their father's hands to be with them.

All of that is in this prayer of Jabez. God's hand can turn the knobs on doors I can never open. His hand can hold back enemies I can never stand against. His hand can empower me to do today what I can never do in my own strength. We need God's power. We need to pray this prayer—that the hand of God might be on us today.

JABEZ TEACHES US TO *PRAY FOR PURITY*

He concludes his brief petition with this: "Keep me from evil." He is not praying a prayer of *isolation* that God would keep evil from him. Note, this is more a prayer of *insulation*, that is, that God would keep *him* from evil. In essence he is praying, "Lord, guard me, protect me, keep me." He knew that even if God blessed him, enlarged his influence, kept His hand on him, all that was no guarantee that he would not fall into temptation.

Jabez was smart enough to know that if he fell into sin, all his pluses would turn to minuses and all his personal gains would become potential losses. How many times have we noticed how a lifetime of achievement and integrity can be lost in a single moment of sensual pleasure . . . and not because evil came to a person; they went to it. So Jabez then adds, "that I may not cause pain." He sought to prevent grieving others by his own actions.

> Jabez was smart enough to know that if he fell into sin, all his pluses would turn to minuses.

This is an amazing prayer so tucked away within the pages of our Bibles. If we were not aware of the outcome, we might wonder if this wasn't a self-centered petition. But look at the verdict. "So God granted him what he requested." The Lord blessed Jabez. He enlarged his territory and influence.

He kept His hand of blessing on him. And He helped him remain pure and away from evil. And He will do the same for you.

CODE VERSE

"The LORD bless you and keep you; the LORD make His face shine upon you, and be gracious to you; the LORD lift up His countenance upon you, and give you peace." (Numbers 6:24–26)

13 THE PRAYER THAT GETS RESULTS

O God of my father Abraham and God of my father Isaac, the
LORD who said to me, "Return to your country and to your family,
and I will deal well with you": I am not worthy of the least of all
the mercies and of all the truth which You have shown . . . Deliver
me, I pray, from the hand of my brother . . . for I fear him . . . For
You said, "I will surely treat you well, and make your descendants
as the sand of the sea, which cannot be numbered for multitude."

—GENESIS 32:9–12

One of the most moving and heartfelt reconciliations ever recorded in the annals of human history takes place in Genesis 33:4: "Esau ran to meet him [his brother, Jacob], and embraced him, and fell on his neck and kissed him, and they wept." Over twenty years earlier Jacob had cheated his brother, Esau, out of his cherished birthright. Fearing retribution, he ran for his life and lived in exile for two decades, isolated from Esau's threats of retaliation. What caused this amazing change of heart that turned years of hostility into a scene of tears and kisses? It was God moving in the hearts of everyone involved through this prayer of Jacob. Prayer changes things. More importantly, prayer changes people, and people then change things. This is a prayer that gets results.

Initially, Jacob appealed to God on the basis of a sure and established covenant relationship with Him. He addressed the "God of my father Abraham and God of my father Isaac." This unbreakable covenant was established with Abraham (Genesis 12:1–3), repeated to Isaac (Genesis 17:19), and passed down to Jacob (Genesis 28:12–13). Jacob was in a covenant relationship with God Himself. And there is good news—so are we, through the new covenant. We have entered into this unbreakable relationship with Him.

All true prayer begins here where Jacob began, that is, with an acknowledgment of our covenant relationship with God through Jesus Christ. Some pray without seeing results simply because they have never been born into His forever family and entered into a lasting relationship with God, enabling them to approach Him saying, "Our Father."

THE PRAYER THAT GETS RESULTS IS *SCRIPTURAL*

Note Jacob threw himself on God's word and pleaded a promise God had given him earlier, saying, "I am with you and will keep you wherever you go, and will bring you back to this land" (Genesis 28:15). Now in his prayer he stood on that Bible promise as he addressed God as "the Lord who said to me, 'Return to your country and to your family, and I will deal well with you.'" Jacob stood on God's personal promises

> Your Bible is filled with God's promises to you; find one, stand on it.

when he prayed. Your Bible is filled with God's promises to you; find one; stand on it. The prayer that gets results is based on the promises of God.

THE PRAYER THAT GETS RESULTS IS *SINCERE*

Jacob continued, "I am not worthy of the least of all the mercies and of all the truth which You have shown." He was not approaching God in prayer on the basis of his own merit. He avoided a proud position and sincerely acknowledged his total unworthiness before God.

When we realize that God doesn't grant our requests on the basis of who we are or what we may have done, but on the basis of who Jesus is and what He has done, we will come before God as Jacob did and discover when we look around that the throne room of prayer is covered with the blood of Christ and not our own good works.

THE PRAYER THAT GETS RESULTS IS *SPECIFIC*

There are no generalities in Jacob's prayer. He got specific. "Deliver me, I pray, from the hand of my brother, from the hand of Esau; for I fear him." Many pray and see little results because their prayers are filled with nothing more than generalities when God wants us to request specific things from

Him. Jacob told God exactly what his heart desired. For twenty years he had lived under the threat of retaliation, and in an instant God answered his prayer and changed the heart of Esau.

THE PRAYER THAT GETS RESULTS IS *SELFLESS*

Jacob sought no glory for himself. He closed his prayer with a higher motive, an eye to God's own glory. "For You said, 'I will surely treat you well, and make your descendants as the sand of the sea.'" Jacob longed for a reconciliation with his brother so that God would receive glory as His promises to Abraham, Isaac, and himself found fruition in the eyes of a watching world.

God is waiting, willing, even longing to answer your prayers with results that exceed your most optimistic hopes and desires. You can pray with amazing results and see your own prayers miraculously answered, as did Jacob. Make sure you pray on the basis of your established relationship with God through faith in the Lord Jesus. Then stand on His promises, repeat them back to Him, and appeal to Him on the basis of who Christ is and what He has done, not who you are and what you may or may not have done. Be specific when you pray. Lay it out before Him. And keep an eye out for God's glory in the outcome. Our great Lord is far more interested in answering your prayers than you are in asking.

CODE WORD: SAND

The next time you see sand in an hourglass or a beautiful picture of a beach in some tropical setting, let it remind you that God kept His promise to make Abraham's seed as "the sand of the sea" in number. And He keeps His promises to you today.

CODE VERSE

You do not have because you do not ask. (James 4:2)

14 PRAYING THROUGH THE TABERNACLE

*"And there I will meet with you, and I will speak with you
from above the mercy seat, from between the two cherubim
which are on the ark of the Testimony, about everything which
I will give you in commandment to the children of Israel."*

—EXODUS 25:22

$\mathcal{T}$he tabernacle in the wilderness, the precursor to
the magnificent Jewish temple on Mount Moriah in
Jerusalem, played a prominent part in Jewish worship as the
Israelites made their march toward the promised land. The
fact that the tabernacle consumes fifteen entire chapters in
the Bible speaks to the tremendous meaning it must hold
for those of us living today in this dispensation of grace. We
have a tendency to skip past long chapters of Scripture such
as this, especially when they are filled with endless items of
minutia. Yet it is in such places that we often find the greatest
gems in our own spiritual growth and development.

God gave the Israelites explicit instructions for the
construction of this tent of meeting, better known as the
tabernacle. Upon entering the structure, you are first con-
fronted with the brazen altar. Walking past it, you pass the
laver and then enter the actual tent itself. There you find the

table of shewbread and the golden lampstand. Passing these you then come to the altar of incense, and just behind it is the veil. Beyond the veil was the Holy of Holies, containing the ark of the covenant and the mercy seat above it. It was here that God Himself would come to dwell among His people, manifesting His shekinah glory. Long years ago in my own devotional life, I discovered the beauty of praying through the tabernacle. Let's enter it now and begin to make our way toward the Holy of Holies in prayer.

The first stop is the brazen altar. Here the animals were sacrificed, and their blood was shed and sprinkled over the altar. We can never get into the presence of God's glory without first coming to the altar of sacrifice. As we pray through the tabernacle, we make this our first stop to remember the final and complete sacrifice on the cross, which eliminated once and for all the need for further animal sacrifices. Here we bow before the Lord, the Lamb of God. We remember that nothing we have done has brought us access to a holy God in prayer. Only Christ's sacrificial death on the altar of the cross makes our access to God possible. We pray with Paul, "Thanks be to God for His indescribable gift" (2 Corinthians 9:15).

Our next stop is at the bronze laver. Here the ancient priests of Israel would stop to wash and cleanse themselves before entering into the presence of God. As we journey through the tabernacle in prayer, we stop here to remember the truth of 1 John 1:9 that "if we confess our sins, He is faithful and just to forgive our sins and to cleanse us from all unrighteousness." We are now ready to enter into the tent, the Holy Place. But wait—it is only for the priests. And then we remember that Jesus Christ, our High Priest, has made us "kings and priests to His God and Father" (Revelation 1:6). So, through Christ, we may now come boldly into God's presence.

> Through Christ, we may now come boldly into God's presence.

Next, we pause a moment at the table of shewbread. Here were placed twelve loaves of bread, one for each tribe, which were offered to God through the week. Pausing here reminds us of our need for "daily bread" ourselves, the Word of God. We remember that the Bible and prayer go hand in hand. Prayer without the Bible has no direction. So we stop here in our prayer time, open our Bibles, and listen for God's voice.

Moving on we come next to the beautiful golden lampstand. It held seven lamps, and since there were no windows in the tent, it provided the only light. When we stop here along the way of our prayer walk, we are reminded that Jesus is the Light of the World and the only One who can bring light to our darkened lives. We are reminded that the light we use to discern and discover His truths comes only from Him.

Next, we find ourselves at the altar of incense. Incense was always burning on this altar and lifting a sweet-smelling aroma toward heaven. Here is found our life of sweet communion and prayer with God through Jesus Christ. The incense reminds us that the Holy Spirit, our prayer partner, is praying through us and for us. Here we pray that our very lives might become a "sweet-smelling aroma" to the Lord Himself (Ephesians 5:2). We began at the cross, stopped for a fresh cleansing through confession of our sins, feasted on the bread of His Word, relied on the light He shines on His Word, and have lifted our praise like incense to Him. Now, we are ready to step beyond the veil into the Holy of Holies.

Once we enter this sacred space, we find ourselves at the ark of the covenant. Before us is the most sacred of all the pieces of furniture in the tabernacle. It contained the tablets of the Law given to Moses, a pot of manna that fell in the wilderness, and Aaron's rod that budded. And above it and between the two gold angelic figures was the mercy seat, where the blood was sprinkled to atone for the sins of the people. And once this was accomplished, the glory of God would fill the Holy of Holies as His very presence visited His people. Here we are reminded that because of the sacrifice of Christ, we too are standing now in the very presence of Christ, who "always lives to make intercession for [us]" (Hebrews 7:25).

In the tabernacle in the wilderness we find one of the Bible's most expressive and informative pictures of the way into His very presence. Make this prayer journey a part of your daily prayer life and you, like the ancient high priests of Israel, will find your very self immersed in the presence of God.

CODE WORD: MAP

Today, when you pull up a map on your smartphone or look at one on the navigation screen in your automobile, let it be a reminder that embedded in the Bible account of the tabernacle is a route of prayer that will lead you to your destination, the very presence of God Himself.

CODE VERSE

Not with the blood of goats and calves, but with His own blood He entered the Most Holy Place once for all, having obtained eternal redemption. (Hebrews 9:12)

15 A PRAYER FOR SERVICE

Here am I! Send me.

—ISAIAH 6:8

*W*hat a different world we would have if every believer expressed from the heart this prayer of Isaiah of old, "Here am I! Send me." This passionate response is given to a penetrating question from the Lord—"Whom shall I send, and who will go for Us?" (Isaiah 6:8). But this question and the prophet's immediate response did not simply issue out of a whim. It is preceded by a series of revelations that came to Isaiah. He awakened to three realities that moved and motivated him to pray this prayer to be used by God to make a difference in his world. We, like Isaiah, will make this our prayer when, like him, we begin to see God, ourselves, and those around us in a new and powerful way.

GOD'S HOLINESS

This prayer, "Here am I! Send me," begins when we *see God in His holiness*. Isaiah was given a glimpse of the Lord "high and lifted up" (Isaiah 6:1). He heard the music of heaven as the angelic choir sang, "Holy, holy, holy is the LORD of hosts" (v. 3). This incredible vision of what awaits all believers led him to exclaim, "My eyes have seen the King, the LORD of hosts" (v. 5). King Uzziah, their earthly king, had just died, and most everyone's eyes were focused on the state of affairs swirling around them. But Isaiah had been privileged to peer into heaven, and he saw our great God "sitting on a throne, high and lifted up" (v. 1). While Israel's earthly king had died and his throne was empty, Isaiah realized that God had not abdicated His throne and that He was still large and in charge.

Worship is not about us. It is not about what we do, what we sing, what we say. It is about almighty God and His glory. The first step in a desire to be used by God is when we, like Isaiah, see God in His own holiness and recognize and realize, no matter what our earthly situation may be, He is in total control.

OUR HELPLESSNESS

This prayer, "Here am I! Send me," becomes a reality for us when we not only see God in His holiness but when we *see ourselves in our helplessness*. Isaiah's first response to his glimpse of God's glory was to express, "Woe is me, for I am undone! . . . for my eyes have seen the King" (v. 5). Too often we never move into the service of being used by God because we measure ourselves by the wrong standard. We tend to compare ourselves to those around us. Instead,

> As soon as Isaiah "saw the Lord," he realized the hard truth about himself.

we are called to look at our own lives in relation to righteous standards of God's law and His own righteousness. As soon as Isaiah "saw the Lord," he realized the hard truth about himself.

Isaiah did not try to sweep his sinfulness under the rug. His immediate response was akin to Job's when he said, "I have heard of You . . . but now my eye sees You. Therefore I abhor myself, and repent in dust and ashes" (Job 42:5–6). The same response came from Peter when he witnessed the Lord's majesty and exclaimed, "Depart from me, for I am a sinful man, O Lord!" (Luke 5:8). And don't forget aged John, who saw the glory of Christ on his lonely island of exile called Patmos, and his first response was, "I fell at His feet as dead" (Revelation 1:17).

When we see the Lord in His glory and holiness like Isaiah, we immediately see ourselves differently and join him saying, "Woe is me . . . I am undone!" And when we confess our own helplessness to Him, we hear the same pronouncement Isaiah heard, "Your iniquity is taken away, and your sin purged" (Isaiah 6:7). Then we are able to hear God's clear voice asking of us what He then asked of Isaiah, "Whom shall I send, and who will go for Us?" (v. 8).

OTHERS' HOPELESSNESS

But there is one thing more. We will make Isaiah's prayer to be used by God our own when we *see others in their hopelessness*. Only after coming to a fresh realization of God's holiness and his own helplessness apart from the Lord, only after his confession brought a fresh cleansing from his sin, did Isaiah see clearly God's call to service. And, only then did he offer his prayer, "Here am I! Send me." He did not say, "Here I am." That would have merely indicated his physical location. But praying, "Here am I" revealed Isaiah's willingness to serve. This was followed with a passionate request, "Send me." God responded with an immediate assignment, "Go, and tell this people" (v. 9). Isaiah had a job to do. He asked for it.

God is still asking this question of those who are called by His name today: "Whom shall I send, and who will go for Us?" Catch a fresh glimpse of who God really is and you will see yourself for who you really are. Then, with true confession and repentance, you will, like Isaiah, find a new beginning and hear clearly His voice asking, "Whom shall I send?" And, once you hear it, make Isaiah's prayer your very own: "Here am I! Send me."

CODE WORD: CHURCH

The next time you are in a worship service in your local church setting, ask yourself three questions. *Have I seen the Lord in His holiness? Have I seen myself in my helplessness? Have I seen others in their hopelessness without Christ?* If you can answer yes to these three questions, you will know you have truly worshiped. And your immediate response will be, "Here am I! Send me."

CODE VERSE

Jesus said to them again, "Peace to you! As the Father has sent Me, I also send you." (John 20:21)

16   JUST A CALL AWAY

*"Call to Me, and I will answer you, and show you great
and mighty things, which you do not know."*
—JEREMIAH 33:3

id you know that God has a telephone number? It is Jeremiah 33:3, and He invites you to call Him anytime—and He promises to always answer. But there is more; when you call on Him, He will show you amazing things that have never even entered your mind. This verse holds one of the most amazing promises in all the Bible. When you call Him, His line is never busy. You never get put on hold. You never have to listen to a voice message. You never get a quick text reply saying, "Sorry. I can't talk right now." He never fails to answer your call—and He answers in a way that far exceeds your most hopeful and optimistic expectations.

Prayer, this ability to fellowship with God, is one of the awesome privileges of the Christian experience. It is of particular interest to note that the only thing the disciples ever asked Jesus to do was teach them to pray. Their request was pointed: "Lord, teach us to pray" (Luke 11:1). They heard Him preach powerful sermons, but they did not ask Him to teach them to preach. They watched Him engage numerous men and win in personal evangelism, but they never asked Him to teach them to evangelize. They sat at His feet and heard Him teach the most marvelous life lessons anyone ever heard, but they never asked Him to teach them to teach. They saw the way He wisely organized and mobilized the crowds, but they never asked Him to teach them to do that. Their only recorded request of Him was to teach them to pray. They had eaten with Him, slept with Him, spent day and night with Him for three years. They witnessed the intensity and frequency of His own personal prayer life with the Father. They watched Him as He went up into the mountains to pray, as He sometimes prayed through the night, as He prayed before every great undertaking, as He prayed after every great victory; and, thus, they knew if they could ever capture the essence of prayer, they would have no problem preaching, teaching, or performing any of the other tasks their ministries would need accomplished.

"Call to Me." What a simple invitation. God invites you into His throne room of prayer. We are not referring here to reciting ancient prayers of other people by rote or through rituals. We are talking heart-to-heart communication with the One who knows what we have need of before we even ask.

Prayer is two-way communication. It is not one-sided. Prayer is the talking part of a relationship. To have a positive and productive relationship with our wives, husbands, children, parents, fellow workers, or whomever else, there must be verbal communication. An early sign that a relationship is souring is a lack of communication between the two parties. Yet some believers seem to think they can go days or even weeks without communicating with God in prayer and still lead effective and fruitful Christian lives.

> Prayer is the talking part of our personal relationship with the Lord.

Prayer is the talking part of our personal relationship with the Lord. And, just think about it . . . He initiates it. He invites you to "Call to Me."

And when we make this call to Him, we have His promise—"I will answer you!" No ifs, ands, or buts. No voice mail. No being put on hold. He picks up every single time you place the call.

The Lord knows far better than we do the deepest needs of our hearts. It is prayer that makes God real to us. Just as reading our Bible gives direction to our prayers, our prayers bring a new dynamic to our Bible reading. God speaks to us through His Word, and we speak to Him through prayer.

So much of heaven will be filled with music. Prayer is like a symphony when you think about it. The Bible is the score. The Holy Spirit is the conductor. You and I are the instruments. As we immerse ourselves in God's Word, the Holy Spirit directs and leads us in our prayer lives, and we actually pray scriptures for ourselves and for others.

Jesus is always our example—in all things. This includes time alone in prayer with our heavenly Father. If He who never sinned realized the need to pray so often, how much more do we, sinful as we are, need to call on Him and rest in His promise that He will answer our prayers? Jeremiah 33:3 is one of hundreds of prayer promises we find on almost every page of the Bible.

But there is more. "Call to Me . . . and I will answer you . . . and show you great and mighty things which you do not know." He will let us see it. He will "show" us some things we do not know. But not just some things, "great and mighty things." If we truly could grasp the depth of this verse and stand on its promise, there is no end to what God could and would do through our lives for His glory and our good. He will not just answer your prayers in some nebulous way. He is waiting and willing to *show* you "great and mighty things."

I have memorized many of my family's and friend's phone numbers. Memorize God's phone number today—Jeremiah 33:3. Then call Him. He will answer, every single time. And He has something big to show you.

CODE WORD: MUSIC

Today, when you listen to music on your radio or phone, let it remind you that prayer is like a symphony. The Bible is the score. The Holy Spirit is the conductor. And you are the instrument. He will guide you into what you need to pray.

CODE VERSE

"I know the thoughts that I think toward you, says the LORD, thoughts of peace and not of evil, to give you a future and a hope. Then you will call upon Me and go and pray to Me, and I will listen to you." (Jeremiah 29:11–12)

17 A PRAYER OF DESPERATION

O LORD, how long shall I cry, and You will not hear?
—HABAKKUK 1:2

*T*his question asked by Habakkuk was born out of a "burden" that consumed him (Habakkuk 1:1). He faced a moral dilemma. How could a holy and loving God—who had called Israel the "apple of His eye" (Deuteronomy 32:10)—now allow the pagan, godless Babylonians to besiege and ultimately destroy the city of Jerusalem? If we are honest, most of us have felt like this at one time or another. We, too, have been burdened by what seems the inactivity of our God on our behalf. We too have bombarded the throne of God's grace with our cries and prayers for deliverance, only to feel as if they were bouncing right back at us from off the ceiling. Yes, at one time or another, who of us has not prayed, "O LORD, how long shall I cry, and You will not hear?"

If a good and all-powerful God really does exist, why doesn't He answer our prayers for what we are convinced are good and right requests? Why does He continue to allow so much evil and suffering? It is the age-old skeptics' argument—either God is all-powerful but not all good (therefore He does not stop evil in its tracks) or He is all good but not all-powerful (thus He is powerless to stop the evil swirling around us). This seems on the surface so logical. If, in fact, He is really all-powerful, then He could eliminate all evil, pain, and suffering in an instant. Let's suppose for a moment He were to decree to do that, to eradicate all evil at midnight this evening. But is that such a wonderful idea? If He were to do that, do you realize that not one of us reading these words, not to mention the one typing them now, would be around at 12:01 a.m.? Jeremiah, the very one who warned of the coming captivity in Babylon, reminds us that our hearts are "deceitful . . . and desperately wicked" (Jeremiah 17:9). I, for one, am extremely grateful that "He has not dealt with us according to our sins, nor punished us according to our iniquities" (Psalm 103:10).

God has not stood idly by. In fact, He has done something dramatic about the problem of evil in our world. He did the costliest and the most loving thing possible; He sent and surrendered His own Son to die in the place of sinful human beings like us.

Habakkuk left us a book in the Hebrew Bible consisting of only three brief chapters, but in them the prophet discovers and reveals to us that the real issue at hand is not evil, but the direction of our own prayer focus.

FOCUSING *ON* CIRCUMSTANCES

Some people place their prayer focus *on* their present circumstances. This is Habakkuk's consuming prayer focus in the first chapter of his book. It is expressed in His prayer, "O LORD, how long shall I cry, and You will not hear?" Again, at one time or another, his cry of desperation has been our own. "Where are You, God? Why don't You do something?"

> "Where are You, God? Why don't You do something?"

When unfair circumstances are swirling all around us and we place the focus of our prayers on them, it leads us to ask these questions that have no satisfactory answers. There is a better way to focus in prayer than by placing all our attention *on* our circumstances and situations.

FOCUSING *THROUGH* CIRCUMSTANCES

Some people place their prayer focus *through* their present circumstances. The prophet changes his focus in chapter 2 when he climbs up on a watchtower to "watch to see what He will say to me" (Habakkuk 2:1). He begins to focus his prayers *through* his present challenges instead of *on* them.

Perspective is vital in our prayer life. Habakkuk began to look at the issue at hand from God's perspective and not his own. This was the secret of Joseph's prayer focus in Genesis, when his brothers sold him into slavery and a series of difficult situations ensued. From the human perspective, nothing that was happening to him could be good or fair in any manner. Jealousy is wrong. Betrayal by your own brothers is wrong.

Being sold as a slave is wrong. Being thrown in prison on a trumped-up charge is wrong. But when he was revealed to his brothers, he looked them in the eye and said, "Do not therefore be grieved or angry with yourselves . . . for God sent me before you to preserve life" (Genesis 45:5). He added, "You meant evil against me; but God meant it for good" (50:20). How could he say this? His prayer focus was *through* his present circumstances, not *on* them.

Placing his prayer focus through his circumstance led Habakkuk to conclude chapter 2 saying, "The Lord is in His holy temple" (Habakkuk 2:20). His focus led him to understand that God had not abdicated His throne, that in and through it all, He was still in charge.

FOCUSING *BEYOND* CIRCUMSTANCES

Finally, some people place their prayer focus *beyond* their present circumstances. We find the prophet closing his book with these words: "Though the fig tree may not blossom, nor fruit be on the vines . . . the olive may fail . . . the fields yield no food . . . the flock may be cut off . . . no herd in the stalls . . . Yet I will rejoice in the Lord, I will joy in the God of my salvation" (Habakkuk 3:17–18).

This is the same man who, three brief chapters earlier, was shaking his fist in the face of God and blaming Him for his desperate dilemma. What changed? In a word, focus; his prayer focus. The same thing can happen to you who are tempted to question, accuse, and even blame God for what may feel like His coldness to you. Stop focusing your prayers *on* your circumstance and put your prayer focus *through* them. If you will do this, you will begin to focus your prayers *beyond* your present problems. Then you, like Habakkuk, can find the comfort only God can bring to your heart.

CODE WORD: FOCUS

Today, when you are focusing in on some small print you are attempting to read, let it be a reminder of the importance of focusing in prayer. Make sure your prayer focus is not *on* your circumstance, but your prayers are focused *through* and *beyond* them.

CODE VERSE

The vision is yet for an appointed time; but at the end it will speak, and it will not lie. Though it tarries, wait for it; because it will surely come, it will not tarry. (Habakkuk 2:3)

18   A PRAYER OF REJOICING

Mary said, "My soul magnifies the Lord, and my
spirit has rejoiced in God my Savior."

—LUKE 1:46–47

*L*uke's gospel opens with an introduction to a carefree young teenage girl playing in the streets of Nazareth one day, and the next day discovering she is pregnant, even though in her words she asked, "How can this be, since I do not know a man?" (Luke 1:34). The visiting angel was quick with the answer: "The Holy Spirit will come upon you, and the power of the Highest will overshadow you; therefore, also, that Holy One who is to be born will be called the Son of God" (v. 35). Mary, realizing that the long-awaited Messiah was now alive and growing in her very womb, began to pray. Her first impulse was not to fear she would be misunderstood by all those who knew her, or to fear when she began to show in her pregnancy that she might become the brunt of every barroom joke in her hometown; but her first impulse was to pray. She began to explode in a prayer of praise and rejoicing. Her impulsive prayer emerged from her soul ("my soul magnifies the Lord") and it emanated from her spirit ("my spirit has rejoiced in God my Savior").

There is a difference between the soul and the spirit.

While they are both used to describe that part of us that is immaterial, they are not always synonymous. We derive our English word *psychology* from the root of this Greek word translated "soul" in Luke 1:46. Your soul is the seat of your emotions. The soul is what connects us to each other on the human level. It is also what gives life to the body. Without it the body dies and decays.

The spirit, on the other hand, is what connects you with God in the spiritual dimension. With the soul we are alive physically, and it is with our spirit that we come alive spiritually when we put our faith and trust in Jesus Christ. The soul comes alive when we are born. The spirit comes alive when we are born again.

PRAYER FROM THE SOUL

Mary's prayer *emerged from the soul*. Upon hearing that she was the chosen one to be the mother of the Messiah, her first impulse was to give praise to God—"My soul magnifies the Lord." To magnify means to celebrate, to acknowledge greatness. Mary had every reason to feel a bit proud. But she never did. Her only thought was of God's greatness. Try and put yourself in her place. God has chosen you for the most special assignment of all mankind. Your cousin Elizabeth has boasted that you are blessed above all women (Luke 1:42). The human reaction would be to take a bow, to take some credit. Not Mary. She fell to her knees and her first impulse was to glorify God with every fiber of her being, her very soul.

PRAYER FROM THE SPIRIT

Mary moves on in her prayer. It didn't just emerge from the soul. This prayer *emanated from the spirit*. The young virgin now moves from the soulish realm (that part of her that connects with man) to the spiritual realm (that part of her that connects with God)—"My spirit has rejoiced in God my Savior." When we are saved through faith in Christ alone, the spirit is quickened and comes alive in us. No wonder one of our first expressions is to rejoice with "joy inexpressible and full of glory" (1 Peter 1:8). Since God is a Spirit, Scripture teaches us that to worship Him, we must do so in "spirit and truth" (John 4:24).

Our spirit, that part of us that connects with God and will live as long as He lives, is what differentiates us from all the other created order. Take your pet, for example. Animals may have a body and, in a sense, a soul, a seat of emotions. That is, they have feelings and their own personalities. But there is nothing about them that can connect with the God of the universe, spirit to Spirit, as we can. We, on the other hand, have the capacity to "rejoice in God our Savior" through the spiritual realm. To know Him is to love Him and to rejoice in the salvation He has provided for us.

Why is magnifying God and rejoicing in Him the point of Mary's prayer? She knows that God is personal, has been mindful of, and has "regarded [her] lowly state" (Luke 1:48). She also recognizes His mighty power as she continues, "For He who is mighty has done great things for me" (v. 49). She also acknowledges that this great God is pure—"Holy is His name" (v. 49). And, she reminds us, He is patient—"His mercy is on those who fear Him" (v. 50). Thank God for His mercy, which is best defined as "not getting what we deserve."

> He is long-suffering and patient toward us. Aren't we grateful?

He is long-suffering and patient toward us. Aren't we grateful? He lets us start all over again when we need to do so. No wonder upon the birth of the babe, the angel came with "good tidings of great joy" (Luke 2:10).

Your soul is designed to "magnify the Lord" before all those you touch in the normal traffic patterns of life. And it is no wonder that your spirit, that part of you that will live forever, continually rejoices in "God our Savior." Worship is the "thank You" that refuses to be silent. It is that voluntary act we offer to Christ our Savior. So join Mary in her prayer. Go ahead: pray it for yourself—"My soul magnifies the Lord, and my spirit has rejoiced in God my Savior."

CODE WORD: PET

Today, when your dog or cat snuggles up next to you in your favorite chair or sofa, let it remind you that you are a special creation of God, indescribably valuable to God. You have a body. You have a soul. And you have a spirit with which you can connect with the Creator God of the entire universe through Jesus Christ our Lord.

CODE VERSE

Bless the LORD, O my soul; and all that is within me, bless His holy name! (Psalm 103:1)

19 PRAYER AND THE HARVEST

When He saw the multitudes, He was moved with compassion
for them, because they were weary and scattered, like sheep
having no shepherd. Then He said to His disciples, "The harvest
truly is plentiful, but the laborers are few. Therefore pray the
Lord of the harvest to send out laborers into His harvest."
—MATTHEW 9:36–38

*C*omfort zones: we all have them, those areas of life from which we seldom stray. Some are social, some economic, others political, and still others religious. It becomes easy to settle in, get comfortable, and never venture out beyond these boundaries many of us set in life. The gospel is a call for us to leave our comfort zones and see "the multitudes" through the eyes of Jesus today.

This is exactly what our Lord did. Talk about leaving a comfort zone. He stepped away from the safety and security of heaven, left the praise of the angelic hosts, and came to earth to encase Himself in a body of human flesh and walk in the midst of publicans, sinners, religious phonies, the despised and rejected of society, and the multitudes who, in His own words, are like "sheep having no shepherd." His call to us then, and now, is to see "the multitudes . . . with compassion." Yes, to move out of our own comfort zones.

On a given day, while in the normal traffic pattern of His preaching and teaching ministry, the Bible records how upon seeing the multitudes of people, Jesus was "moved with compassion for them, because they were weary and scattered." These men and women were weak and exhausted from the daily struggles of life under Roman oppression. They were beaten down, with no hope and no direction, weary and scattered. They are still here, all around us. Many of them are holding on to life by a thread. We look, but do we see? When we begin to see them through the eyes of Jesus, we too will be moved with compassion and find the motivation to move out of our own predetermined and predisposed comfort zones.

Jesus' emphasis in this passage is on what He calls "the harvest." It is full. It is ready. There is an energy and urgency behind His call to the harvest. It is not a call to plow the fields. It is not a call to plant the crops. It is not a call to prepare and cultivate. Jesus focuses on the "harvest." But He quickly acknowledges there is a major problem—"the laborers are few." Not the spectators. There are lots of them. God's problem today is not out there in the fields. They are ready. They are plenteous. They are ripe. They are waiting. Things haven't changed much in two thousand years; God's problem is still with His own people.

So here we are, like the disciples, often just content in our own snug little comfort zones. The multitudes are all

> So here we are, like the disciples, often just content in our own snug little comfort zones.

around us; they are weary and without spiritual direction; they are ripe to be harvested. But few are willing to go into the fields and bring them in. So, what are we to do? Human reasoning says get a plan, enlist the workers, beg, plead, coerce if necessary, strategize, find a catchy theme, pull out all your best motivational techniques, and, if needed, even try guilt for motivation.

But God has a better way. Jesus says, in light of all this, "Therefore, *pray.*" Jesus moves prayer to the very top of the priority list when it comes to evangelism and the harvest. We should not lose sight of the fact that this was always Jesus' priority. Before He chose the Twelve, He spent the entire night in prayer. Luke records the event for all posterity: "Now it came to pass in those days that He went out to the mountain to pray, and continued all night in prayer to God. And when it was day, He called His disciples to Himself; and from them He chose twelve whom He also named apostles" (Luke 6:12–13). If time and space permitted, this could be illustrated again and again. Prayer was the priority of our Lord . . . always.

It is important to note the object of His prayer in Matthew 9 for the harvest. We automatically surmise that it is in the direction of the poor lost souls needing direction and hope. But it is not. Jesus calls us to focus our prayers on

God sending out the "laborers." He calls on God to "send out laborers into His harvest." This is not a subtle, passive appeal. The New Testament word we translate "send out" is a strong, active word indicating a violent motion. This is not some little powder puff toss. Behind this Greek word is the thought of haste and urgency. When it comes to the harvest of the lost world around us, Jesus is not calling us to organize and recruit people to be on our team. This is a call to pray. And for what? For God to move into action, thrusting you and me from our very comfort zones and into the harvest field of personal evangelism. After all, it is *His* harvest, and the laborers are sent by Him on mission.

Earlier Jesus had revealed to these disciples that the fields were "already white for harvest" (John 4:35). My first pastorate was in the wheat farming community of Hobart, Oklahoma. Being a city boy, I was enthralled by the wheat harvest that consumed the entire area for those short weeks in late May and early June each year. You could drive for miles and see nothing but golden waves of grain like a vast bronze ocean spreading across the horizon. I asked one of those farmers about this verse. Jesus said the fields were "white" to harvest and yet all I could see was "amber waves of grain." He quickly explained that when the wheat started turning white, it was almost too late to get it out. You had to move with all urgency before it rotted in the field.

Yes, the harvest fields around us today are "white for harvest." There will not always be adequate time. This is a time for us to leave our comfort zones and put our priority where Jesus did—*pray* . . . to the Lord . . . to send out laborers . . . into His field. In all our talk of evangelism and the need to reach those who are lost, let us remember that prayer is our priority, always in all ways.

CODE WORD: POLITICS

Today, when you talk politics with your friends or family, ask yourself how many are on "the other side" of your viewpoints. Let it remind you that Jesus' call is for us to leave our comfort zones, whether they are social, economic, racial, or political, and to always keep prayer our priority.

CODE VERSE

Rejoice always, pray without ceasing, in everything give thanks; for this is the will of God in Christ Jesus for you. (1 Thessalonians 5:16–18)

20   LISTEN TO HIM

While He was still speaking, behold, a bright cloud overshadowed
them; and suddenly a voice came out of the cloud, saying, "This
is My beloved Son, in whom I am well pleased. Hear Him!"
—MATTHEW 17:5

*M*any of us share a common fault in our conversations with others. So often, we fail to listen.
We are so immersed in preparing to articulate our next
brilliant thought that we are prone to not hear what the
other person is saying. How many times have we been
introduced to someone and as soon as we walk away cannot even remember the person's name? On the mountain
of transfiguration, the Father gives us some good advice.
He introduces His Son, affirms His pleasure in Him,
and then admonishes us to "listen to him" (Matthew
17:5 ESV).

One of the things we often forget about prayer is that it
is communication with the Lord. And communication is a
two-way street. We talk . . . and, if we are smart, we listen
even more than we speak. Perhaps one of the most overlooked and forgotten elements of prayer is taking the time
to listen to Him. He still speaks to us through His Word and
by His Spirit. God is essentially saying to us here, "This is

My Son; I love Him; I am pleased with Him. Stop talking so much and listen to Him."

After the resurrection, Jesus showed up on the road to Emmaus to perfectly illustrate this need in all of us to take time in prayer to stop talking and simply "listen to Him." For three years the disciples had walked with Christ, talked with Him, virtually lived with Him, when suddenly it all came to an abrupt and crashing conclusion: Jesus had been viciously executed and His body tossed in a cold, damp tomb. Then, all the disciples "forsook Him and fled" back to their own abodes (Matthew 26:56).

Two of these followers headed home to Emmaus, a village seven miles west of Jerusalem. As they walked in discouragement toward the sunset that afternoon, they exclaimed to one another, "We were hoping that it was He who was going to redeem Israel" (Luke 24:21). But they had buried that hope when the body of Jesus was placed in the tomb of Joseph of Arimathea. Dejected and dismayed, they were walking proof that there is never power in the present when there is no hope in the future.

But, then—suddenly—the resurrected "Jesus Himself drew near and went with them," but they "did not know Him" (Luke 24:15–16). After this incredible encounter "their eyes were opened and they knew Him; and He vanished from their sight" (Luke 24:31). And their response? "Did not our heart burn within us while He talked with us on the road?" (Luke 24:32). Isn't this one of our most pressing needs today? That is, burning hearts that come from listening to Him along our own Emmaus road.

> "Did not our heart burn within us while He talked with us on the road?"
>
> LUKE 24:32

LISTEN TO HIM AS HE SPEAKS TO US THROUGH HIS SPIRIT

Their hearts were set on fire when "He talked with [them] on the road." Jesus was doing the talking, and they were doing the listening. Their hearts did not burn when they talked to Him, or when they talked to each other about Him. Their hearts began to burn with a new passion when they stopped talking to Him and to others and started listening to Him, spirit to Spirit.

There comes a time when we need to stop trying to perform, stop offering our petitions, even cease our praise for a moment, and simply be still and listen to His still small voice speaking to our spirits, and heed the admonition of our heavenly Father to "listen to Him."

LISTEN TO HIM AS HE SPEAKS TO US THROUGH HIS SCRIPTURE

The Bible remains a sealed book until God's Spirit opens its truth to us. We may gain a head knowledge of Him through the Bible, but we will never be able to understand a heart knowledge, a spiritual discernment, until, like the disciples, He talks to us along the road and opens the Scriptures to us (v. 32). And we do the listening.

Jesus "expounded" to them in all the Scriptures the things that concerned Himself (v. 27). The word *expound* connotes the thought of translating something out of a foreign language. The Bible is really a foreign language to those who do not believe. "Beginning at Moses . . . He expounded to them in all the Scriptures the things concerning Himself." From the Pentateuch to the Prophets Jesus preached Jesus. From Moses to Malachi He revealed how the entire Jewish Bible speaks of Him. As He spoke to them, a shadow of the cross fell over the Jewish Bible. He was that ram at Abraham's altar in Genesis. He was the Passover lamb in Exodus, whose spilled blood meant freedom from slavery and deliverance from death . . . and still does. He was that scarlet thread out Rahab's window in Joshua. And the good shepherd of whom David spoke in the Psalms? Jesus was that shepherd. As the disciples listened, they understood that Jesus was the suffering servant spoken so eloquently about by Isaiah. And He was the fourth man in the midst of the fiery furnace in Daniel. No wonder their hearts began to burn within them. He was doing the talking . . . and they were doing the listening.

The disciples' immediate response was noteworthy. They

"rose up that very hour and returned to Jerusalem" to exclaim to all the others, "The Lord is risen indeed!" (vv. 33–34). Their glowing hearts turned into going hearts. With beating, burning hearts they scurried back to Jerusalem, around the corners, down the narrow alleys, up Mount Zion, to find the others and share the good news. And they shared it not with an emaciated question mark, but with a bold exclamation mark: "He is alive!"

One of these Emmaus followers was named Cleopas. His companion is left unnamed. I like to think this is so in order for you and me to find ourselves in his or her place as we walk on our own road today. Perhaps you are reading these words with your own hopes dashed and your own dreams smashed. Stop. Look. Listen to Jesus' Spirit through His Scriptures. He is still speaking. And if you listen, you just might walk away with your own heart burning within you. "Listen to Him."

CODE WORD: CELL PHONE

Today, when your phone rings and you answer and begin listening, let it remind you that prayer is a two-way conversation also. Stop doing all the talking; listen to Him!

CODE VERSE

A voice came out of the cloud, saying, "This is My beloved Son. Hear Him!" When the voice had ceased, Jesus was found alone. But they kept quiet. (Luke 9:35–36)

21 THE PATTERN OF PRAYER

Lord, teach us to pray.

—LUKE 11:1

*I*n our modern world we have tools at our disposal that our parents never dreamed of having. Take the navigation systems on our cars and smartphones. We simply type in the address of our destination and it guides us there, telling us where to turn, how far we have to go, and even gives us an estimated time of arrival. When the disciples asked our Lord to teach them to pray, they were asking for a route, a path, that would lead them into the throne room of God's presence in prayer. The Bible clearly lays out this route for us, and it begins when we pray the prayer of confession.

THE PRAYER OF CONFESSION

The Bible reveals that our sins have separated us from God "so that He will not hear" (Isaiah 59:1–2). King David lamented, "If I regard iniquity in my heart, the Lord will not hear" (Psalm 66:18). Thus, it is obvious that the place to begin in prayer is to come clean and confess our sins to Him while standing on His promise that "if we confess our sins, He is faithful and just to forgive us our sins and to cleanse us from all unrighteousness" (1 John 1:9). Spend a moment confessing your sins to the Lord. Perhaps there are sins of the tongue, things you may have said. Perhaps sins of action, something you may have done that transgressed His law and will for your life. What about sins of thought? It is not a sin to have a certain thought pass through your mind. It becomes one when you do not allow it to do that—to pass through—and you harbor it in your heart. There are also sins of omission, things we did not do that we knew we should have done. The Bible warns that "he who covers his sins will not prosper." However, the same verse promises that "whoever confesses and forsakes them will have mercy" (Proverbs 28:13).

> The place to begin in prayer is to come clean and confess our sins to Him.

THE PRAYER OF THANKSGIVING

Once we have confessed our sin, we now can move on to a time of giving thanks. The Bible says, "Enter into His gates with thanksgiving, and into His courts with praise" (Psalm 100:4). You can never enter the throne room of prayer until you first come through the gate of thanksgiving. At this juncture in our prayer time, we pause to thank God for material blessings: our home, our car, our shoes, and all that we have. We then give thanks for our physical blessings: eyes, mind, hearts, health. Next, we thank God for particular people in our lives who cause us to be better than we might be otherwise. Finally, we thank Him for spiritual blessings like love, joy, peace, and our own salvation. Thanksgiving has a liberating effect. Remember, it was when Jonah offered a prayer "of thanksgiving" that he was liberated from his predicament in the belly of a fish (Jonah 2:9–10).

THE PRAYER OF PRAISE

Once we have entered through the gate of thanksgiving, we can now stand in the "courts with praise" (Psalm 100:4). Here we pause to let Him know how much we love Him as we answer the question He once asked of Simon Peter, "Do you love Me?" (John 21:15). Here we praise the Lord for His attributes: His goodness, patience, mercy, holiness, love. While we thank God for what He does, we praise Him for who He is.

THE PRAYER OF INTERCESSION

After confessing our sin, giving thanks, and offering praise, we now move to the prayer of intercession. This is the prayer in which we approach the Lord in prayer on behalf of someone else. Here we pray for our family members, pastors, missionaries, friends, political leaders, and so on. I have, through the years, found great joy in praying for those who may have spoken or come against me in some form or fashion. During this time of intercession, we pray for those we may know who do not know the Lord. Here we realize that the person without Christ is blind to the things of the Lord, for "if our gospel is veiled, it is veiled to those who are perishing, whose minds the god of this age has blinded, who do not believe, lest the light of the gospel of the glory of Christ, who is the image of God, should shine on them" (2 Corinthians 4:3–4). Therefore, realizing that "the weapons of our warfare are not carnal but mighty in God for pulling down strongholds" (2 Corinthians 10:4), we intercede in their behalf pulling down strongholds of pride, prejudice, presumption, procrastination, or any stronghold in which we discern they may be held, thus freeing them to choose Christ.

THE PRAYER OF PETITION

After the prayers of confession, thanksgiving, praise, and intercession, we come to the prayer of petition. Here we ask God for anything and everything that He may have placed on our hearts. We are to delight ourselves in the Lord, and He will give us the desires of our hearts (Psalm 37:4). This does not mean that whatever our hearts may desire He will give us. But it does mean that those desires in our hearts will have been implanted there by Him. He gives and grants the desires that originate at His own throne.

THE PRAYER OF COMMUNION

After journeying through this pathway of prayer, we come to the place of communion with Him. Here we are simply quiet before Him with an open Bible, listening to His "still small voice" speaking to us at a point of our need (1 Kings 19:12). When my wife, Susie, and I first met, we talked profusely on those first few dates, not wanting the other to think we were boring. But after we had been dating awhile, we would sit in my car in front of her parents' home after a date and not say a word for a good while . . . but we were communicating at a personal level! The prayer of communion is the prayer we pray that goes beyond mere words when we just sit still before Him and listen.

As you begin to journey through prayer using this route, you, who perhaps have not been able to pray more than five minutes, will find that you will be praying longer and more powerfully than you ever dreamed possible.

CODE WORD: NAVIGATION

Today, when you use your navigation system to get you to a specific destination, let it be a reminder to you that the Bible lays out the route of prayer. Begin with confession; then proceed on to thanksgiving, praise, intercession, and petition, and you will end up in the sweet destination of the prayer of communion.

CODE VERSE

"You will seek Me and find Me, when you search for Me with all your heart." (Jeremiah 29:13)

22

THE ORIGINAL LORD'S PRAYER

"Father, the hour has come. Glorify Your Son, that Your Son
also may glorify You . . . I have manifested Your name to
the men whom You have given Me out of the world . . . Keep
[them] through Your name . . . that they may be one as We
are . . . I do not pray for these alone, but also those who will
believe in Me through their word; that they all may be one . . .
And I have declared to them Your name . . . that the love with
which You loved Me may be in them, and I in them."

—JOHN 17:1–26

On my personal calendar are certain dates marked in the future for which I am compelled to make preparation before that time comes. For Jesus, "the hour has come." His reference to this "hour" relates to the date marked on God's calendar of eternity when Jesus would become the sacrifice for our sin and would hang suspended between heaven and earth on a Roman cross. He and His band of followers had left the upper room and walked to the garden of Gethsemane. There, Jesus prayed as they listened intently to the most passionate and revealing conversation between God the Father and God the Son recorded in all the Bible.

Jesus prays for Himself, revealing who He is. Next, He

prays for His disciples, revealing who they were. Finally, He closes His prayer praying for you and me, along with all those in the coming generations who would believe in Him, revealing who we can be. While the model prayer of Matthew 6 is often, and erroneously, referred to as "the Lord's Prayer," this high priestly prayer of Jesus recorded by John in his gospel can lay exclusive claim to being the original "Lord's Prayer."

JESUS PRAYS FOR HIMSELF

What would be the center and object of your prayers if you were faced with execution in a matter of hours? Jesus focused His prayer for Himself on what He considered the two most important matters at hand—God's glory and God's grace.

Our Lord's primary motivation, in and through the cross, was for the Father to receive glory. He prayed, "Glorify Your Son." But why? "That Your Son may glorify You." One of the keys in Bible study is to always look for this little conjunction *that*. Then ask the question, "Why?" Here Jesus prays, "Glorify Your Son." Then, He adds "that." And we ask why. The next phrase tells us: "that Your Son may glorify You." For Jesus, praying for Himself involved making sure God the Father was glorified in all He did.

Jesus was also focused on God's grace. Hear Him give a definitive definition of mission on earth—"And this is eternal life, that they may know You, the only true God, and Jesus

Christ whom You have sent" (John 17:3). He was consumed not in His own welfare but in God's grace, His unmerited favor, being bestowed on all who would believe. He followed this with a declaration—"I have finished the work which You have given Me to do" (v. 4). No wonder, a few hours later, we would hear His final words from the cross, "It is finished!" (John 19:30). In His hour of greatest need, His prayer for Himself was consumed with God the Father receiving glory and His grace being freely distributed to all who would believe.

> In His hour of greatest need, His prayer for Himself was consumed with God the Father receiving glory.

JESUS PRAYS FOR HIS DISCIPLES

Put yourself in their place. They knew what loomed ahead. And now they listened as He poured out His heart in prayer . . . for them. When I read these words, I wonder what dynamic impact it would have on me to hear Jesus praying for me right now in the next room. I think I would not fear a thousand foes if that were true. And yet, He is praying for you and me this very moment. The Bible says, "He always lives to make intercession" for us (Hebrews 7:25).

In their moment of greatest need Jesus prayed for their security and their purity. He beseeched the Father to "keep [them] through Your name." After acknowledging that "the world has hated them," He shared His parting desire: that the Father would keep them safe to share the gospel with a waiting world (John 17:14). He was focused not only on their security but also on their purity. He asked the Father to "keep them from the evil one" (v. 15). He wasn't praying that they would be isolated from the world, but that through the Word they would be insulated from Satan's attack. He concluded His prayer for them with a plea that they would be "sanctified by the truth" (v. 19). They had the task of taking His gospel to the whole world, and Jesus prayed that they would be secure and pure in doing so.

JESUS PRAYS FOR US

Yes, that is right. The night before He was crucified you were in His thoughts and prayers. The focus of His prayers for us is that we would be together, "that they all may be one." And that we would be together, forever!

Jesus' heart's desire is that believers become "one." Why? Here is that little conjunction *that* again—"that they also may be one in Us, *that* the world may believe that You sent me" (v. 21). The result of believers living in love and unity, together, forever, is that others might be drawn to Christ.

Jesus concludes this amazing petition asking that "the love with which You loved Me may be in them, and I in them." What amazing love is in each of us who believe. And there is more—Jesus Christ Himself is alive in everyone who believes. Jesus is still praying that we will be together (one with Him and one with each other), forever.

CODE WORD: CALENDAR

Today when you look on your calendar, remember that for Jesus "the hour had come." He was ready for it. But before He rushed out to the grim hill of Golgotha, He knelt in the green garden of Gethsemane and prayed for you and me. He still desires all His followers to be together forever.

CODE VERSE

There is neither Jew nor Greek, there is neither slave nor free, there is neither male nor female; for you are all one in Christ Jesus. (Galatians 3:28)

23   PRAYING WITH POWER

They raised their voice to God with one accord . . . "Now,
Lord, look on their threats, and grant to Your servants that
with all boldness they may speak Your word, by stretching
out Your hand to heal, and that signs and wonders may be
done through the name of Your holy Servant Jesus."

—ACTS 4:24–30

*J*esus was gone . . . physically. The disciples had watched the agony of the crucifixion, been with Him during those post-resurrection days when He remained in His glorified body, had watched Him ascend back into heaven from the Mount of Olives, and, now, living with the hope that He was going to return soon, they came under tremendous persecution. Peter and John were arrested and upon their release were commanded by the authorities "not to speak at all nor teach in the name of Jesus" (Acts 4:18). It was the worst of times and the best of times for the early church. Thousands of people were being swept into the kingdom of God through the witness of the disciples and the church (three thousand are recorded in Acts 2 and another five thousand are recorded in Acts 4). The early church was exploding in growth.

The fourth chapter of Acts reveals one of the greatest

prayer meetings in all of history. The secret of the early church was that they were a people of prayer. And they knew how to pray with power and get results. A close observation of this particular prayer meeting reveals three secrets to

> The secret of the early church was that they were a people of prayer.

praying with power. Prayer power involves being scriptural, being specific, and being submissive.

When Peter and John were released from prison, they went straight to their companions and reported what had happened. The group's first inclination was not to plan or plot what to do next, but to pray. They threw themselves on the sure Word of God and took their stand upon it.

PRAYER POWER IS SCRIPTURAL

Prayer power involves *being scriptural*. Prayer and the Bible go hand in hand. Prayer without the Bible has no direction. And, conversely, the Bible without prayer has no dynamic.

Their prayer for power begins by standing on God's Word, specifically Psalm 2:1–2. Hear them pray, "Lord, You are God . . . who by the mouth of Your servant David have said: 'Why did the nations rage, and the people plot vain things? The kings of the earth took their stand, and the rulers were gathered together against the LORD and against

His Christ'" (Acts 4:24–26). They found their strength and the answer to their dilemma in the Word of God. They realized that this is exactly what God said—seven hundred years earlier, through David—would happen. The "kings of the earth" (Herod), the "rulers" (Pontius Pilate), the "nations" (the Gentiles, Romans) and the "people" (the Jews).

Praying the Scriptures in such a fashion brought them to see that God was in charge. Their prayer continued, acknowledging that what was happening was only because of what "Your hand and Your purpose determined before to be done" (v. 28). These early believers prayed with power because they knew the Scriptures and used them when they prayed. They offered the Word back to God. They stood on it. They believed it. They claimed its promises as their own. Nothing enables the believer to pray with power like Scripture memory and standing on God's Word when we pray. It brings the authority and power of heaven into the spiritual bankruptcy of men and results in power.

PRAYER POWER IS SPECIFIC

Not only does prayer power involve being scriptural but, also, *being specific*. Their immediate future looked bleak. They were the object of threats, imprisonments, beatings, even death. The Lord had warned them that in the world they would have tribulation (John 16:33). So how would they now pray? This was no time for generalities, a "God help us, God bless our work." They prayed specifically for two things, courage and confirmation.

They prayed for *courage*—"Grant to Your servants that with all boldness they may speak Your word" (Acts 4:29). They realized that their greatest danger was not from without but from within. So they didn't flee to some monastery to escape the world; they prayed to be bold. They needed supernatural courage to overcome their fears.

They referred to themselves as "servants," bondslaves. They had given up their own rights so as to come under the control of their Master. Now their specific request was not to flee their adversaries with cowardice but to face them with boldness and courage.

They also specifically prayed for *confirmation*—"that signs and wonders may be done through the name of Your holy Servant Jesus" (v. 30). They asked God to confirm their new faith with miraculous manifestations that superseded human explanation. And He did! There is much the modern church can learn from this prayer meeting in Jerusalem two thousand years ago. God honors prayers that are scriptural and specific. Dare to ask Him for what only He can do. Be specific when you pray.

PRAYER POWER IS SELFLESS

Power in prayer also results in our *being selfless* when we pray. These men and women were far more concerned with honoring Christ than they were their own reputations. They put themselves aside. They were cautious not to take any credit, acknowledging that it was only "through the name of Your holy Servant Jesus" that their victories were achieved (v. 30). It is noteworthy that we never find Simon Peter or any of the early believers approaching God on the basis of their own merit, but solely in the name of Christ. They were wise enough to know that the Father did not grant their requests on the basis of who they were or what they had done but on the basis of who the Lord Jesus is and what He has done.

These early believers never asked God to remove their problems from them, but to give them a new boldness in confronting them. God may not remove your problem from you, but if you will pray with power, He will give you the grace to deal with it. Be scriptural when you pray. Find a Bible promise and stand on it. Claim it as your own. Be specific. Pray with faith. And be selfless. Seek Christ's highest good and desire that in and through all things He will be glorified.

CODE WORD: IGNITION

Today, when you start the ignition of your car, let it be a reminder to you of the power that mighty engine ignites and so remind you that there is power in prayer—scriptural prayer, specific prayer, selfless prayer.

CODE VERSE

Through the hands of the apostles many signs and wonders were done among the people. And they were all with one accord in Solomon's Porch. (Acts 5:12)

24   WHAT HAPPENS WHEN PEOPLE PRAY?

When they had prayed, the place where they were assembled
together was shaken; and they were all filled with the Holy
Spirit, and they spoke the word of God with boldness. Now
the multitude of those who believed were of one heart and
one soul; neither did anyone say that any of the things he
possessed was his own, but they had all things in common.

—ACTS 4:31–32

*T*he early church faced their difficulties and challenges
not with protests or politics but with prayer that resulted
in powerful living. The preceding verses to our text present
one of the most dynamic and instructive prayer meetings in
recorded history. Verse 31 begins, "When they had prayed . . ."
Can we, two thousand years removed from them, expect the
same things to happen when we pray with power as they did?
There are five manifestations resulting in the scriptural, specific, and selfless prayers we find recorded in Acts 4.

WHEN WE PRAY, *WE BEGIN TO PERCEIVE THE PRESENCE OF GOD*

The place where they had gathered was "shaken." They knew
God was there in the midst of them! They perceived His very

presence. Note the order. It was when they had prayed that the place was shaken, not when the place was shaken they began to pray. It might well be that the very reason we often do not sense His presence with us is that we wait until something around us is shaken before we begin to pray.

It is possible to become so involved with good things, godly things, that we actually lose a sense that God is near and like Jacob later have to confess, "Surely the LORD is in this place, and I did not know it" (Genesis 28:16). But when we pray as the early believers prayed, it becomes atmospheric.

WHEN WE PRAY, *WE BEGIN TO RECEIVE THE POWER OF GOD*

The Bible records that "When they had prayed . . . they were all filled with the Holy Spirit." God's power in our lives comes through prayer. Yesterday's experience never suffices for today's commitment. Prayer is new every morning. And so is His filling of our lives.

In the Ephesian epistle Paul admonishes each of us to "be filled with the Spirit" (Ephesians 5:18). Then in the next three verses, he lays out the obvious proof that God's Spirit is filling us. There is an inward evidence—"singing and making melody in your heart to the Lord." There is an upward evidence—"giving thanks always for all things." And there is an outward evidence—"submitting to one another."

So much of what happens in our churches today can be explained with human plans and programs. But our greatest need is power. And power comes only through prayer.

WHEN WE PRAY, *WE BEGIN TO ACHIEVE THE PURPOSE OF GOD*

Why does the Spirit fill us? So that we might speak the Word of God with "boldness." This is God's purpose for every believer, to share the gospel. Listen to some of the Lord's last words to us before He ascended back into heaven: "But you shall receive power when the Holy Spirit has come upon you; and you shall be witnesses to Me . . . to the end of the earth" (Acts 1:8). We receive the power of God for the express reason that we might share His glorious gospel with the entire world.

> Why does the Spirit fill us? So that we might speak the Word of God with "boldness."

In one generation this early church got exactly what they prayed for. Without the means of radio, television, printing presses, the internet, or any of the modern means of communicating the gospel at our disposal today, they took the gospel from Jerusalem all the way to the seat of Roman power and shook it to its core. When we pray as they prayed, we too can begin to achieve God's purpose for us in our generation.

WHEN WE PRAY, *WE BEGIN TO BELIEVE THE PROMISES OF GOD*

It was the multitude of those "who believed" who were of "one heart and one soul" and with "great power . . . gave witness" of Christ to the world (Acts 4:32–33). They believed in the promises God had given them in His Word and took their stand on them. After all, "faith comes by hearing, and hearing by the word of God" (Romans 10:17).

Unity is the single most effective element of a praying church. Believing God's promises resulted in them being of "one heart and one soul" (Acts 4:32). In fact, our Lord said that this is precisely the issue in showing the world that He was sent by the Father. In His high intercessory prayer the evening before the crucifixion, He prayed "that they all may be one, as You, Father, are in Me, and I in You; that they also may be one in Us, that the world may believe that You sent Me" (John 17:21).

WHEN WE PRAY, *WE BEGIN TO RELIEVE THE PEOPLE OF GOD*

One of the by-products of praying with power was that "they had all things in common. And with great power the apostles gave witness to the resurrection of the Lord Jesus. And great grace was upon them all" (Acts 4:32–33). Being Christ's hand extended to those in need is the natural response of a life that is saturated and permeated with prayer.

We will know we have prayed with power when we—like our spiritual forefathers in Jerusalem—begin to sense that God is near, live in His power, are about the business of His purpose, stand firmly on His promises, and have a heart to help and heal those among us in need.

CODE WORD: STAND

Today, when you stand in front of your mirror, getting yourself ready for the day, let it be a reminder to stand on the promises of God. They are personal and powerful.

CODE VERSE

Faith comes by hearing, and hearing by the word of God. (Romans 10:17)

25 A PRAYER FOR DIRECTION

Lord, what do You want me to do?

—ACTS 9:6

*S*ome of the most informative and instructive prayers are those shot like arrows from hearts that are desperate. Paul, who almost single-handedly took the gospel to the far reaches of the known world and left us half of our New Testament through his writings, was not always a dynamo of a Christian leader. Originally known as Saul, he began as the very antithesis of what we know of him today. As a "Jew of Jews" he saw the new Jesus movement as a threat to all he had known and sought to preserve. He became the point person assigned with putting down this exploding phenomenon. In Acts 8, his terrorist cell, operating in Jerusalem, had successfully eliminated Stephen, the first Christian martyr. He was engaged in a high-intensity campaign of intimidation and murder to crush this new and expanding church movement.

While en route to Damascus to stamp out a Christian uprising there, something happened that forever transformed him. "Suddenly a light shone around him from heaven. Then he fell to the ground, and heard a voice saying to him, 'Saul, Saul, why are you persecuting Me?'" (Acts 9:3–4). It was none other than the risen Christ miraculously appearing to him. Then, "trembling and astonished" he asked, "Lord, what do You want me to do?" (v. 6). This became the burning desire of his life—to know God's direction and do what pleased the Lord. Whether experiencing his shipwreck at Malta, being stoned and left for dead at Lystra, suffering beatings and imprisonment in Philippi, and finally being beheaded outside the city gates of Rome, this prayer, "Lord, what do You want me to do?" became the driving motivation of his life.

This question is the prayer every believer should be constantly asking: "Lord, what do You want me to do?" Somewhere there is something for you to do that no one else can do quite like you can do. There is a purpose for your life that, according to Jeremiah, existed even before you took your first breath. Through the prophet's pen God framed

> This question is the prayer every believer should be constantly asking: "Lord, what do You want me to do?"

it, "Before I formed you in the womb I knew you; before you were born I sanctified you; I ordained you a prophet to the nations" (Jeremiah 1:5). Like Jeremiah and Paul, you too have a God-given purpose that should move you to pray, "Lord, what do You want me to do?"

Putting this question into practice in our own experience will require asking two questions: *Who?* and *What?*

The first question to ask of ourselves is, "Who?" Note the order of the personal pronouns in Paul's question. *You* comes before *me*! Too many of us pray something to this effect: "Lord, here are my marching orders for You today. Bless me; take care of my family; meet this need for me; straighten out this other person." This results in a "What have you done for me lately?" attitude. But a new day will dawn on your Christian experience when you put Christ first and begin each day praying, "Lord, what do *You* want *me* to do today?"

Remember this truth—He knows you . . . always has . . . always will . . . everything about you. He did not simply know you were in the womb. There is nothing remarkable about that. Anyone could have concluded that along the way of your mother's pregnancy. But God knew you even before you were conceived. You are no accident. No one on this planet has a fingerprint or DNA like yours. God has a specific, tailor-made design for your life. If this is true, who of us would not want to find that kind of direction in life? And who of us would not want to pray, "Lord, what do You want me to do?" The "who" is important. It is not about you; it is all about Him. It is not about what you want to do, but it is all about what God wants you to do that matters most in life.

Next comes the question of "what?" Paul asked, "*What*

do You want me to *do*?" The answer comes in realizing that God did not simply know you before you were born, but He set you apart and has a job for you to do that no one else can do as well as you can. Just as God "ordained" Jeremiah and Paul to a specific task, He has uniquely assigned you a specific assignment. This word we translate "ordained" is from the Old Testament word that means "to assign; to designate." Interestingly, the same word is used in the first chapter of the Bible when we read how God "set [the stars] in the firmament" (Genesis 1:17). Each one of the millions of stars has its own appointed place set by God, and they all move in clocklike precision. Just as God has set and assigned each single star, He has assigned each and every one of us a job to do. True success in life comes not in simply knowing what God's plan is for us but in doing it.

Make this prayer of Paul's your daily prayer. When you do, you just might find it as life-transforming as he did. Go ahead—pray it now: "Lord what do *You* want *me* to *do*?" And when you pray like this, you have the promise of God: "You will show me the path of life; in Your presence is fullness of joy; at Your right hand are pleasures forevermore" (Psalm 16:11).

CODE WORD: STAR

Tonight, step outside for a moment and look at the stars in the heavens. Let them remind you that God set each of them in place. In the same way, He knows you and has a wonderful plan for your life. He will not keep it from you when you pray from a sincere heart, "Lord, what do You want me to do?"

CODE VERSE

I will instruct you and teach you in the way you should go; I will guide you with My eye. (Psalm 32:8)

26   GOD IS LISTENING

Peter was therefore kept in prison, but constant prayer
was offered to God for him by the church.

—ACTS 12:5

*H*ave you ever had a time when you simply did not
know what to do, when it seemed as if hope was
almost gone? The early believers lived in such a moment in
the twelfth chapter of Acts. King Herod was putting tremendous pressure on these Christ-followers. John the Baptist had
been beheaded, Jesus had been crucified, and now James, the
brother of John, was martyred by the sword. Seeing that this
"pleased the Jews," Herod had Simon Peter thrown in prison.

While we do not live in first-century Palestine, we who
follow Christ today are often faced with our own obstacles,
causing us to sometimes feel as if hope is almost gone for us
as well. Many today are living on the edge and wondering if
God is even aware of our need. In these situations there are
some things for us to remember: God is looking. God is listening. God is leading.

GOD IS LOOKING

God knew Peter was in prison (Acts 12:1–4). Never once in
the Bible did Jesus ever come upon a situation and say, "Wow,

that was a surprise!" He is always looking. The Bible says, "The eyes of the LORD run to and fro throughout the whole earth, to show Himself strong on behalf of those whose heart is loyal to Him" (2 Chronicles 16:9). If He sees a sparrow when it falls (Matthew 10:29), how much more is He aware of your every need?

Sometimes we think that no one sees us, that no one cares. But God does. He is looking. He sees you. Simon Peter never got away from this thought. Later he would pen a letter to the dispersed church and, quoting King David, say, "The eyes of the LORD are on the righteous, and His ears are open to their prayers" (1 Peter 3:12). God is looking. He sees everything going on in your life this very moment.

GOD IS LISTENING

It is one thing to know that He is looking, but how wonderful to know He truly hears us. While Peter was incarcerated under heavy guard, Acts 12:5 records, "Peter was therefore kept in prison, but constant prayer was offered to God for him by the church." And God heard them. If this were recorded today, the verse might read, "Peter was kept in prison but the church petitioned on his behalf . . . or lobbied the politicians. . . . or tried to take over the local precinct . . . or picketed on his behalf." Two words—*influence* and *power*—describe the difference in the early church and the modern church. These believers in Acts 12 did not have enough influence to keep Peter out of prison, but they had enough power to pray him out because they were convinced that God was listening.

God is listening to your prayers. You might be prone to say, "Well, if He is listening, He does not seem to be answering." But God always answers our prayers. Always. Sometimes His answer is *direct*. We pray and immediately the answer comes. Sometimes His answer is *delayed*. We pray, and for His own good reasons, God seems to put us in a holding pattern. Then there are times when the answer is *different*. That is, He answers, but in a different and better way than we had anticipated. And finally, there are times when our requests are *denied*. I am grateful God has not answered all my prayers with a yes because there are times I have asked Him for something that in His providence was not best for me at the time. When we pray, we can be sure that God is not only looking; He is listening.

GOD IS LEADING

In answer to the church's prayers, an angel of the Lord came to Peter in the prison and led him out. When they came to the prison door, the "iron gate that leads to the city . . . opened to them of its own accord; and they went out" (Acts 12:10). There are many doors in life that we can open ourselves, but there are some iron gates that are human impossibilities where there is no hope unless He supernaturally opens the door. Some of us face these iron gates of life and beat on them until our knuckles are bloody and bruised, when the only thing that opens them is "constant prayer" to a God who is looking, listening, and leading.

Peter ran to the home where he knew the church was meeting and began to knock on the door. When he identified himself, they still did not open the door. Here God answered their specific prayer, but they couldn't move themselves to believe it. It is interesting that God opened the iron gate of the prison but not the wooden door of the church. Inside, these men and women were in constant prayer. But the fact is, there comes a time for us to stop praying, believe, and go open the door.

> There comes a time for us to stop praying, believe, and go open the door.

God has not abandoned His throne after all these centuries. He is still looking today. Nothing has come your way of which He is unaware or surprised. He sees you . . . this very moment. He is still listening today. His ears are attentive to your prayers. And He is still leading anyone who will believe and follow. Simon Peter went from this experience to the greatest days of his life. He became the undisputed leader of the Jerusalem church before he met his own martyr's death by being crucified upside down, insisting he was unworthy to be crucified in the same manner as his Master. We still have a God who sees us, who is intent on hearing our every request, and who desires to lead us in the path He has chosen for us. God is listening.

CODE WORD: GATE

Today, when you pass through a gate, let it be a reminder that there are some gates in life that are humanly impossible to pass through unless God intervenes. And let it remind you that your great God is looking, listening, and leading.

CODE VERSE

The eyes of the LORD are in every place, keeping watch on the evil and the good. (Proverbs 15:3)

27 FIRST THINGS FIRST

I exhort first of all that supplications, prayers, intercessions, and giving of thanks be made for all men, for kings and all who are in authority, that we may lead a quiet and peaceable life in all godliness and reverence. For this is good and acceptable in the sight of God our Savior, who desires all men to be saved and to come to the knowledge of the truth.

—1 TIMOTHY 2:1–4

ome time ago the pastor of one of the nation's largest churches laid out a vision outlining plans for the next decade of expansion. He was inspiring as his dreams of new buildings and new budgets were placed before the people. The congregation rose to their feet and broke into applause as they heard where the pastor was leading them. But one thing was strangely missing in the entire presentation—there was no mention of the place that prayer would play in this endeavor.

How diametrically opposite was Paul's view of church growth. Listen closely as he instructs young Pastor Timothy: "I exhort *first of all* that supplications, prayers, intercessions, and giving of thanks be made for all men" (emphasis mine). Church-growth books are a dime a dozen in our modern world of performance-driven philosophies. Some are program driven; some are philosophy driven; others are purpose driven. Paul left us several letters in our New Testament amounting to little volumes on church growth. And every one of them is prayer driven.

> The pathway to worship is always through the door of prayer and praise.

The primary purpose of the church is the worship of the Lord Jesus Christ, and the pathway to worship is always through the door of prayer and praise. Paul points us in this chapter to prayer's urgent priority and to prayer's ultimate purpose.

PRAYER'S URGENT PRIORITY

Prayer brings with it an *urgent priority*. When Paul says to Timothy and to us, "I exhort," it is not a simple suggestion. Nor is it a command being forced on us. The word means to call alongside, to plead, to encourage. Paul is saying, "I encourage you. I plead with you. I urge you to see that prayer is your priority." Like a championship coach giving a pep talk right before the big game, Paul is lining up what should be our urgent priority in the Christian life: prayer.

When the apostle says, "First of all," he is saying prayer should be in the forefront of everything we do. The secret to success in the early church was the way they constantly fought to keep prayer as their number one priority. They remembered the words of Jesus, "My house shall be called a house of prayer" (Matthew 21:13). Before it is to be the house of Bible teaching, fellowship, evangelism, missions, or anything else, it is to be known as the "house of prayer."

Paul reminds us that our prayers should consist of "supplications, prayers, intercessions, and giving of thanks." The word translated "supplications" describes an intense, special, personal need. It is a prayer arising out of a burden for something that may be lacking, some special need. It describes those who plead before God in brokenness and tears over the needs of others as well as themselves. Then we are to pray "prayers." In Greek, this word has a reverence attached to it that other synonyms in the prayer family do not have. It describes the manner in which we are to come before royalty. And then, the apostle adds "intercessions" to this priority. The word means we are standing before God on someone else's behalf. What a privilege to meet God on behalf of someone else and lay their needs before His throne. Finally, Paul adds "the giving of thanks." Thanksgiving has a liberating effect. Ask Jonah, who offered a sacrifice of thanksgiving from the belly of the fish and was immediately delivered (Jonah 2:9).

The Bible lays before us here a beautiful expression of prayer on an ascending scale. We come before Him making our requests (supplications), He then leads us to ask for larger blessings (prayers), and then we are bold in standing in the gap for someone else pleading their case (intercessions), which causes our devotion to issue in thanksgiving. Prayer is our urgent priority.

PRAYER'S ULTIMATE PURPOSE

Prayer also brings with it an *ultimate purpose*: to glorify God through the salvation of souls whom Jesus came to save. Paul frames it by saying that God "desires all men to be saved and to come to the knowledge of the truth." This is God's stated desire, His will, and it should be our ultimate purpose.

Prayer was once a priority in our nation. Every morning in my public elementary school we started the day with a prayer over the intercom system. We once believed that prayer could really change things in our lives and world. But prayer has been relegated to the ranks below pickets and protests and politics. The early church never tried to change their world from without with plans and programs but from within, keeping their priority on prayer. And they saw God's ultimate purpose fulfilled in ways that no generation has seen since.

Paul reminds young Timothy what is "good and acceptable in the sight of God our Savior": that God "desires all men to be saved and to come to the knowledge of the truth." This is God's bottom line. This is no guarantee that all will be saved.

They won't. We are not puppets; we are people with the ability to make choices in life. God made us this way because the love we can voluntarily return to Him is indescribably valuable to Him. He sends the Holy Spirit to convict us; He draws us to Himself; His love constrains us; His kindness leads us to repentance. But ultimately, the choice is ours. His heart longs for each of us to know Him and to come to the knowledge of the truth—for when we know the truth, it "shall make [us] free" (John 8:32).

CODE WORD: HOUSE

Today when you leave your house, or this evening when you return to it, ask God to make it a reminder to you that prayer is our urgent priority and carries with it our ultimate purpose. Jesus said, "My house shall be called a house of prayer" (Matthew 21:13).

CODE VERSE

Rejoice always, pray without ceasing, in everything give thanks; for this is the will of God in Christ Jesus for you. (1 Thessalonians 5:16–18)

28 PUT ON THE GOSPEL ARMOR

Finally, my brethren, be strong in the Lord and in the power of His might. Put on the whole armor of God, that you may be able to stand against the wiles of the devil . . . praying always with all prayer and supplication in the Spirit, being watchful to this end with all perseverance and supplication for all the saints.
—EPHESIANS 6:10–11, 18

There is an unseen world all around us. Most believers live oblivious to it. We are more geared to a sense world, what we can see, touch, taste, or smell. But so much is taking place in the atmosphere around us that is totally lost to the physical eye. For example, there are colored pictures and all types of music swirling around us. If we had a television monitor, we could bring them out of the air and into the screen, and the same is true with our radios and music. There is also in this unseen world around us a great cosmic confrontation between the forces of Satan and the forces of God. Satan is constantly at work seeking to lie and deceive us, shooting his arrows of doubt in our direction.

How can we stand against him and his deceptions? Paul admonishes us to "put on the whole armor of God." He is writing this Ephesian epistle from his Roman incarceration. Standing guard over him is a Roman soldier in full armor.

The apostle sees a perfect analogy here and tells us to "put on the whole armor of God" . . . the belt of truth, the breastplate of righteousness, the shoes of peace, the shield of faith, the helmet of salvation, and the sword of the Spirit. Each of these pieces of God's armor, which enables us to "stand against the wiles of the devil," should be put on in prayer. I often begin my own private, personal prayer time in the mornings by going through these verses and making sure, before I face the new day, that I put on this gospel armor, and at each piece I pause to put it on in prayer.

Put on the belt, "having girded your waist with truth" (Ephesians 6:14). The putting on of this belt is not some fashion statement with an expensive Hermès or Gucci belt. For the Roman soldier, the belt was what held everything in place. If he had no belt, his tunic could not be tucked in, his sword could not be sheathed, and his breastplate could not be secured. And this is the belt of what? "Truth." There is no hope in defeating the devil if we do not begin with the truth of the Word of God. It is this truth that holds everything together for us. So, put on the truth of God. Determine to stand each day in His truth.

Put on "the breastplate of righteousness" (v. 14). Next, in our prayer time we pause here to make sure we have this breastplate in place. The breastplate covered the heart and protected the vital organs of the soldier. This is what

Christ's imputed righteousness does for us. Earlier, Paul had reminded the Corinthians, and us, that God "made Him who knew no sin to be sin for us, that we might become the righteousness of God in Him" (2 Corinthians 5:21). It is not our own righteousness that protects us. We must put on the breastplate of His righteousness and stand in it each day.

Next, we make sure our feet are shod with "the preparation of the gospel of peace" (Ephesians 6:15). Any soldier, or any kid who has ever had a youthful playground skirmish, knows you never get in a fight barefooted. Shoes are critical, and these shoes to which Paul refers are the shoes of "peace." There can never be outward peace with others in our lives until we have an inward peace with ourselves. And this is impossible without an upward peace that comes in a relationship with Christ, who is our Peace.

> There can never be outward peace with others in our lives until we have an inward peace with ourselves.

Now, it is time in our prayer journey to take up "the shield of faith" (v. 16). It is the shield that wards off the enemy's arrows, which, often dipped in pitch, came as flaming darts of fire at the ancient warriors. What is our shield? It is our faith. When Satan hurls his flaming arrows of doubt, imaginations, accusations, and the like at us, we lift up our shield of faith against him. Since "faith comes by hearing, and hearing by the word of God" (Romans 10:17), if he shoots an arrow of guilt at us, we hold up our shields, saying, "There is therefore now no condemnation to those who are in Christ Jesus" (Romans 8:1). If the arrow comes in the form of a past sin, we hold up our shields, saying, "He is faithful and just to forgive us our sins and to cleanse us from all unrighteousness" (1 John 1:9). The shield of faith is the persistent application of our faith rooted in the truth of God's Word.

Next, we put on the "helmet of salvation" (Ephesians 6:17). This is the part of the armor that protects our minds and keeps our thinking straight in days of combat and confrontation. So often, the real battle takes place in our minds, in our thinking processes. We need God to "guard [our] hearts and minds through Christ Jesus" (Philippians 4:7).

Finally, now dressed in full battle array, we take up the "sword of the Spirit which is the word of God." Note carefully: the sword is the only offensive weapon listed. All the other pieces of armor are for defense. The Word of God is the most powerful weapon we possess, and when used properly defeats any and all enemies. This is what happened to Jesus when tempted by the devil in the wilderness. Each time He took up "the sword of the Spirit" and answered with the Word of God, saying, "It is written . . ." (Matthew 4:4, 7, 10).

Having put on all the gospel armor, you are now ready to

face anything that might come your way today. The problem lies in the fact that many of us get all dressed for battle and have no clue where the battle is taking place. After describing all the armor, the very next verse tells us where to find the battlefield: "praying always with all prayer and supplication in the Spirit" (Ephesians 6:18). Prayer is the battlefield of the Christian life. Put on the gospel armor. Each piece, put on in prayer.

CODE WORD: SHOES

Today when you get dressed and sit to put on your shoes, let it be a reminder to you of the importance of putting on each piece of this spiritual armor before you leave your house and enter the realm of a real cosmic confrontation. And remember, prayer is the battlefield of the Christian life.

CODE VERSE

Faith comes by hearing, and hearing by the word of God. (Romans 10:17)

29 PRAYER IS THE BATTLEFIELD OF THE CHRISTIAN LIFE

*. . . praying always with all prayer and supplication
in the Spirit, being watchful to this end with all
perseverance and supplication for all the saints.*
—EPHESIANS 6:18

Having "put on the whole armor of God" in the preceding verses, the believer is now ready to do battle with the Enemy. But it is impossible to win a war if you do not know where the battle is being fought. Many believers are fighting the battle today on the field of politics or plans or procedures or programs, or any number of other places. In Ephesians 6, there is no period between verse 17, where we take up our sword, and verse 18, where we pray. Many believers are defeated in life because they do not know where the battle is even taking place. Here the scripture is plain. Prayer is the battlefield of the Christian life. It is here in verse 18 that the battle is fought: "praying always with all prayer . . . with all perseverance . . . for all the saints."

As you read and reread this verse, an obvious truth leaps from this page, revealing four "alls." Paul says we are to pray with all prayer, at all times, with all perseverance, for all the saints. Girded in truth, with the shield of faith, and holding in our hands and hearts the sword of the Spirit, the Word of God, we are now ready to do battle.

VICTORIOUS PRAYING IS *COMPREHENSIVE*

Paul admonishes us to pray with "all prayer." We have seen in this volume that there are many different kinds of prayer providing a pathway into God's presence. For some, the only prayers they pray are prayers of petition, sporadic prayers to help get out of a tight spot or to acquire something they need. Others are so introspective that their prayers are consumed with confession and a feeling of false guilt.

Paul is telling us that when we pray, we are to use all the elements of prayer in our arsenal. This involves the prayer of confession. After all, "if I regard iniquity in my heart, the Lord will not hear" (Psalm 66:18). The prayer of thanksgiving follows. Thanksgiving has a liberating effect on us. We are to "enter into His gates with thanksgiving" (Psalm 100:4). Next comes the prayer of praise. Having entered into prayer through the gate of thanksgiving, we now enter "into His courts with praise" (v. 4). Now we are ready, clothed in all the armor of God, to pray the prayer of intercession. Here we bring to the Lord anyone and everyone He brings before our hearts and minds. The prayer of petition follows. Here we make our "supplications," which are specific requests for the personal matters that weigh on our hearts. Finally, there is the prayer of communion, simply being still with our open Bibles, listening to His still small voice speaking to us. Prayer is the battlefield of the Christian life, and it involves our praying with "all prayer."

> Prayer is the battlefield of the Christian life, and it involves our praying with "all prayer."

VICTORIOUS PRAYING IS *CONTINUOUS*

We are not simply to pray with all prayer but at all times, "praying always." This does not mean we are to pray 24/7, but we are to stay in unbroken communion with the Lord even when there are no words being spoken. This is such a God consciousness that our life becomes one great continual communion with Him.

This attitude can be accomplished in many ways. I have made it a practice each time I hang up the telephone to pause and offer a prayer for whomever I have been engaged with. Kids at school can use the bell that rings numerous times during the day to signal them to pray for someone. Folding clothes is a good time to pray for each family member whose clothes are being folded. All through the Bible we hear this concept of praying at all times. Jesus said, "Watch . . . and pray always" (Luke 21:36). The early church gave themselves "continually to prayer" (Acts 6:4). Paul instructed the Thessalonians to "pray without ceasing" (1 Thessalonians

5:17). What a difference it makes to pray with all prayer at all times.

VICTORIOUS PRAYING IS *COURAGEOUS*

Paul says we are to pray with "all perseverance." That is, we are to never give up, to come boldly before the Lord in prayer. Prayer is warfare. We are reminded of that a few verses earlier—"For we do not wrestle against flesh and blood, but against principalities, against powers, against the rulers of the darkness of this age, against spiritual hosts of wickedness in the heavenly places" (Ephesians 6:12). The testimony of many is revealed in the first five words of this passage, "For we do not wrestle." Again, prayer is warfare. It is a battle. When you enter the battlefield of prayer with all prayer at all times, make sure you add "with all perseverance" to your battle plan.

VICTORIOUS PRAYING IS *COLLECTIVE*

It involves praying collectively for "all the saints." This includes those who may have spoken against you or wronged you in some way. One of my greatest blessings through the years has been found in praying for those who may have spoken against me. Praying for "all the saints" is closely akin to what Jesus did when all those men and women who had been with Him for three years "forsook Him and fled" in His time of greatest need (Mark 14:50). They were included in His prayer from the cross, "Father, forgive them, for they do not know what they do" (Luke 23:34).

I have stood in the very dungeon in Rome where Paul wrote some of his prison epistles. It was damp and dark with just a small ray of light, the ancient iron rings of confinement still embedded in the walls. It was holy ground. Paul was there, but he was free. Make his words a part of your own prayer life. Pray with all prayer . . . at all times . . . with all perseverance . . . for all the saints. You will never win the war unless you know where the battle is being fought.

CODE WORD: TELEPHONE

Today, when you hang up from a phone call, let it be a reminder to pause a moment and pray—with all prayer, at all times, with all perseverance, for all the saints, and for that one to whom you have just been talking.

CODE VERSE

"As for me, far be it from me that I should sin against the Lord in ceasing to pray for you." (1 Samuel 12:23)

30 PRAYING FOR THE SICK

Is anyone among you sick? Let him call for the elders of the church, and let them pray over him, anointing him with oil in the name of the Lord. And the prayer of faith will save the sick, and the Lord will raise him up.

—JAMES 5:14–15

The letter of James in our New Testament was primarily addressed to the believers who fled from Jerusalem under great persecution. His words are amazingly relevant to our world today. We, too, live in the midst of a world of hurts. Hearts are hurting. Families are hurting. Have you looked around you lately in our broken culture? People are sick—not just physically but mentally, emotionally, and spiritually. Thus the question of James is extremely pertinent to our culture—"Is anyone among you sick?"

Perhaps no other ministry of the church has seen as much perversion as that of praying for the sick. While many involved in so-called healing ministries have wonderful intentions and pure hearts, others have too often been used as a vehicle for building personal kingdoms by offering false hopes of healing to any and even all who come their way. Here in the book of James we find the only directive in all of Scripture as to how to pray for the sick.

Contextually, James is describing a local church ministry at a member's bedside. There is no talk here of renting city auditoriums featuring flashy, fancy preachers prancing around while helpless and often hopeless seekers wait in healing lines. This is a ministry of prayer for those in need, and James is explicit in how it is to be accomplished.

THE PROBE

He asks, "Is anyone among you sick?" The key here is understanding what is behind this New Testament word we translate "sick." James carefully chooses a Greek word that means "without strength, to be weak." It is not just physical sickness being addressed here. It applies to those who are weak in body, soul, or spirit. James says that the "prayer of faith will save the sick." Here the word for "sick" means to literally grow weary.

James is writing to those who have grown weary in the struggles of life, those "scattered abroad" (James 1:1). These men and women had been forced to leave their jobs, to flee their homes under the dispersion. They were tempted to give out and give up. They were weary and weak. While these verses can apply to those physically sick, the context indicates they were addressed primarily to those about to crack mentally under the pressures of life.

THE PROPOSAL

James proposes that they "call for the elders of the church." Those who need a healing hand often need someone on whom they can lean and from whom they can draw strength. Note, the initiative is to be taken by those who are sick themselves. The onus is on the sick ones, not the church leaders, to take the initiative.

In response to this invitation, the elders are instructed to perform this ministry of encouragement to, as Paul exhorted, "comfort the fainthearted, uphold the weak, be patient with all" (1 Thessalonians 5:14).

THE PROCEDURE

When a sick person reaches out, the procedure then is for the church to "pray over him, anointing him with oil in the name of the Lord." There are two distinct Greek words we translate into our English word *anoint*. One refers to an outward anointing: literally, "rubbing down with oil." This word is found in the story of the good Samaritan, who bandaged the wounded man, "pouring" oil and wine into the wounds to fight the infection and soothe the hurt (Luke 10:25–37). The other word has more to do with a ceremonial type of anointing used in a sacred and symbolic sense. For example, Jesus used this word to explain how the Spirit "anointed" Him to preach the gospel (Luke 4:18).

Most of what we see in healing ministries today is this ceremonial use of oil in anointing the forehead of a sick person, applying a couple of drops of oil in a symbolic way, often in the sign of a cross. While there is nothing wrong with doing this, it is nowhere near what James is describing. He used the word akin to what the Samaritan did. In other words, James is saying do what you can medicinally to soothe the wound and heal the hurt; use the best medicine known to man. The church should support the efforts of the medical community, and the medical community should welcome the healing efforts of the church by recognizing the power and importance of the "prayer of faith."

> The church should support the efforts of the medical community, and the medical community should welcome the healing efforts of the church.

THE PRAYER

This prayer for the sick is called the "prayer of faith." Earlier in his letter James reminds us that when we pray, we must believe, asking "in faith, with no doubting, for he who doubts is like a wave of the sea driven and tossed by the wind" (James 1:6).

Furthermore, this prayer of faith should always be offered according to God's Word and His will. The prayer of faith is always grounded in the Word of God or it is not a prayer of faith. Paul makes this plain, saying, "Faith comes by hearing, and hearing by the word of God" (Romans 10:17).

THE PROVISION

"The prayer of faith will save the sick, and the Lord will raise him up." Do not think this verse is a carte blanche for healing. It is a package wrapped up in the mystery of God's will and way. Paul himself once repeatedly prayed for healing from his "thorn in the flesh" only to discover when it was not removed that God's grace was all-sufficient (2 Corinthians 12:7, 9).

Physical healing is a mystery wrapped in the counsel of God's own will. Some of God's greatest saints have known some of the greatest sufferings. All healing is divine. Medicine alone doesn't heal. Doctors alone do not heal. Proper diet or exercise alone does not heal. God heals! And our part is to believe and pray with faith that He can still make the impossible possible.

CODE WORD: DOCTOR

Today when you pass a doctor's office or see your own physician, let it remind you that all healing comes from God. The doctor may sew up your wound, but he or she cannot cause the skin to grow together again. You are fearfully and wonderfully made. So pray, and when you pray, pray with the "prayer of faith."

CODE VERSE

"My grace is sufficient for you, for My strength is made perfect in weakness." Therefore most gladly I will rather boast in my infirmities, that the power of Christ may rest upon me. (2 Corinthians 12:9)

31   THE PRAYER THAT AVAILS MUCH

The effective, fervent prayer of a righteous man avails much.

—JAMES 5:16

*J*ames, the half brother of our Lord, who rose to be the leader of the Jerusalem church and gave us the New Testament book bearing his name, lived with a famous nickname that stuck to him as though it were glued to him by the early believers—Camel Knees. He earned that name among his peers because his knees were said to have become calloused and hardened by the time he spent on them in prayer.

In our text, James lays forth the key to "effective" prayer. After all, who among us does not want our prayers to be effective? What mother who pours out her heart in prayer to God for a son or daughter doesn't want it to be effective? What man or woman praying for family or friends who are sick does not long to see their prayers effective? To be effective in our prayer, James reveals that prayer must be approached with integrity and asked with intensity. And when it is, it will be answered with immensity.

EFFECTIVE PRAYER IS *APPROACHED WITH INTEGRITY*

James is talking about the prayer of "a righteous man." On the surface this requirement appears a bit threatening. We are prone to say, "Well, that leaves me out." But James is in no way parading out a few super saints here. All believers are righteous as we stand before God. Paul made this plain: "[God] made [Jesus] who knew no sin to be sin for us, that we might become the righteousness of God in Him" (2 Corinthians 5:21). All of us "in Christ" are clothed in His righteousness, not our own.

However, if this spiritual sense of righteousness is the only thing at issue, why aren't more of our prayers being answered? James is speaking here of moral righteousness. This is the type of integrity that John addressed, saying, "He who practices righteousness is righteous, just as He is righteous" (1 John 3:7). James's emphasis is on *doing* righteousness, not just in *being* righteous. Righteous people are people of integrity. They practice what they preach. John added, "Whatever we ask we receive from Him, *because* we keep His commandments and *do* those things that are pleasing in His sight" (v. 22, emphasis added). Effective prayer is approached with integrity.

EFFECTIVE PRAYER IS *ASKED WITH INTENSITY*

James is not talking about saying your prayers but about saying prayers that are "fervent." We derive our word *energy* from this Greek word. It literally means "stretched out" and is illustrated by a sprinter stretching out toward the finish line with a final burst of energy. Effective prayers take on a powerful and persuasive energy that can be described as "fervent."

> Effective prayers take on a powerful and persuasive energy that can be described as "fervent."

Prayers that get results are not long, drawn-out orations. They are pointed and powerful like that of the publican, "God, be merciful to me a sinner" (Luke 18:13). Or, like Simon Peter, while sinking in the sea, crying out, "Lord, save me" (Matthew 14:30). This was Jacob's prayer when he prayed, "I will not let You go unless You bless me" (Genesis 32:26). They are prayers asked with intensity and approached with integrity.

It is not the length of our prayers but the depth of our prayers that makes them effective. It is not the prayers that issue out of our head, but the prayers that burst forth from our heart that are effective. Approach God with integrity; do those things He commands. Then, pray with passion and intensity. Why? Because "the effective, fervent prayer of a righteous man avails much."

EFFECTIVE PRAYER IS *ANSWERED WITH IMMENSITY*

This prayer "avails much." When we are doing what is right—when we pray in humility with a spirit of energetic fervor—God answers our prayers.

God is still in the business of divinely intervening in the natural process He Himself established. And He does so when we pray with integrity and intensity. God answers prayer. Don't rush past that last sentence. Read it again. God really does answer our prayers. If more of us truly believed this, we might spend more time talking *to* Him than talking *about* Him. God always answers our prayers. There are times when almost immediately we see the answer, just as we prayed. There are also times in which He delays His answer and places us in sort of a holding pattern. Then there have been times in my own life when He has answered, but His answer was not what I had hoped it might be. In fact, some of my prayers have been answered with resounding noes. Yet looking back it was always for my own good and His own glory. And there have been times when He answered my prayer in a different way than I ever would have expected because He always knows what is best for us. But the truth is, God answers our prayers. Always.

May God help each of us to reach up to Him with prayers filled with our integrity and energized by our intensity. And may God help us see that these kinds of prayers "avail much" more than we ever hoped or dreamed.

CODE WORD: ATHLETICS

Today, if you are watching a baseball or football game, each time you see the pitcher reach back and throw a blazing fastball, or a runner stretch to reach the goal line, let it remind you that this type of "fervent" prayer is the kind of prayer that "avails much."

CODE VERSE

Whatever we ask we receive from Him, because we keep His commandments and do those things that are pleasing in His sight. (1 John 3:22)

32   PRAYER AND FASTING

Jesus took him by the hand and lifted him up, and he arose.
And when He had come into the house, His disciples asked Him
privately, "Why could we not cast it out?" So He said to them,
"This kind can come out by nothing but prayer and fasting."
—MARK 9:27–29

*M*ost of us have found ourselves in a similar situation and asked the same question at one time or another in our Christian experience. The disciples had been on a spiritual mountaintop, witnessing the glorious transfiguration of Christ before their very eyes. In the immediate aftermath a man brought his son to them who was possessed by a demon. The disciples did all they knew to do to deliver the lad, but to no avail. In their frustration they asked the Lord a private and pointed question: "What did we do wrong? Why couldn't we cast it out?" We have all been there, praying desperately about a matter of deep concern but seemingly helpless to make a difference. Jesus wanted them, and us, to know that there are certain things along our journey that will come about only when we add fasting to our prayers.

Jesus often linked these two disciplines together. On a grassy green Galilean hillside in the midst of delivering His Sermon on the Mount, He said, "When you do a charitable deed . . . When you pray . . . When you fast" (Matthew 6:2, 5, 16). To Jesus it is always "when," not "if." Our Lord assumes that as believers we will practice fasting just as we do giving gifts and praying. Fasting, the voluntary denial of food in order that God's face may be sought in earnest, persistent, and believing prayer, is one of the forgotten blessings of many modern believers. It is not a command. Jesus never says, "Thou shalt fast." It carries with it no rules, no regulations. It is simply a voluntary discipline that leads the believer to see that every tinge of hunger is but a reminder of the focus of the prayer need at hand. Our Lord joins prayer and fasting together because prayer is one of our hands reaching up to God, while fasting is our other hand letting go for a while of something temporal and visible.

We read a lot of books about prayer today but hear very little about the blessing of fasting. This begs the question, Why, when, and where should we fast?

WHY SHOULD WE FAST?

The most obvious reason is that the Bible teaches it. Over one hundred times we read of those who practiced fasting as a spiritual discipline. Moses fasted when receiving the commandments. David fasted when Saul was slain in battle and when his own child was sick. Elijah fasted after the victory on Mount Carmel. Nehemiah fasted when tasked with the rebuilding the broken walls of Jerusalem. Esther fasted before she was taken before the king. Jonah fasted when he finally headed for Nineveh. Jesus fasted after His baptism in the Jordan. Cornelius fasted when he was searching for the Lord in Caesarea. Paul fasted when he appointed elders in all the churches.

It is amazing that many believers totally ignore the discipline of fasting and know so little about it. And yet Jesus said there are certain things in our lives that come about only by prayer and fasting. If fasting played such an important part in those used by God in the Bible, shouldn't it be a part of our own spiritual growth? We should fast because there are times in each of our lives when the deliberate denial of food helps us focus on the reason for our fast and enables us to concentrate on our petitions before Him.

> If fasting played such an important part in those used by God in the Bible, shouldn't it be a part of our own spiritual growth?

WHEN SHOULD WE FAST?

When devotion needs to be deepened and faith needs to be restored, we should practice prayer and fasting. When there is a particular need before you or someone you love who needs an answer, add fasting to your prayers. We should fast and pray when there are major decisions to be made in life.

This is what the church at Antioch did in Acts 13 when they fasted and prayed and then separated Barnabas and Saul for their first missionary journey. When we need the power of God in our own experience in a fresh and new way, we should add fasting to our prayers. When we need revival, we should follow Nehemiah's ancient example: "So it was, when I heard these words, that I sat down and wept, and mourned for many days; I was fasting and praying before the God of heaven" (Nehemiah 1:4). Who of us doesn't need a fresh touch of God's anointing in our own lives? There are times when this only comes by prayer and fasting.

WHERE SHOULD WE FAST?

This is an important question to ask. That is, should we do so publicly for a witness or privately for God's eyes only? Jesus left no doubt about this. He admonished:

> When you fast, do not be like the hypocrites, with a sad countenance. For they disfigure their faces that they may appear to men to be fasting. Assuredly, I say to you, they have their reward. But you, when you fast, anoint your head and wash your face, so that you do not appear to men to be fasting, but to your Father who is in the secret place; and your Father who sees in secret will reward you openly. (Matthew 6:16–18)

Add a fast to your prayer life. After all, if we believe our Lord, He said, "This kind can come out by nothing but prayer and fasting."

CODE WORD: FOOD

Today when you sit down to lunch or dinner and your food is on a plate in front of you, let it be a reminder to incorporate into your prayer life a time of fasting, perhaps for a meal or a day as a start. Every tinge of hunger will remind you of your reason for your fast and draw you closer to the heart of God.

CODE VERSE

Cornelius said, "Four days ago I was fasting until this hour; and at the ninth hour I prayed in my house, and behold, a man stood before me in bright clothing, and said, 'Cornelius, your prayer has been heard, and your alms are remembered in the sight of God.'" (Acts 10:30–31)

33 PRAYING FOR THE LOST

This is the confidence that we have in Him, that if we ask
anything according to His will, He hears us. And if we
know that He hears us, whatever we ask, we know that
we have the petitions that we have asked of Him.

—1 JOHN 5:14–15

*I*n the early years of my Christian experience, my youth group used to gather to pray for our friends who didn't know the Lord. I remember hearing earnest prayers that went something like this: "Lord, bless Bobby. Lord, speak to his heart. Save him. Help him see the light." And, of course, those prayers always concluded with an "if it be Your will." The struggle was obvious, and the truth is we were praying with sincere hearts the only way we knew to pray.

How do we pray for the lost? As with all prayer, we begin on the platform of seeking God's will. The Bible says, "The Lord is not slack concerning His promise . . . not willing that any should perish but that all should come to repentance" (2 Peter 3:9). That little word *all* is expressly inclusive. The apostle Paul adds, "This is good and acceptable in the sight of God our Savior, who desires all men to be saved and to come to the knowledge of the truth" (1 Timothy 2:3–4). The Bible is plain; God is not desirous that any of us perish and desires for all to be saved. Thus when we pray for our lost friends, we can be sure we are praying from the platform of agreement with the Father's will.

There are three key issues in praying for the lost: we are to pray with the proper approach, the proper aim, and the proper authority.

PRAYING WITH THE PROPER APPROACH

Praying for those who do not know the Lord involves *praying with the proper approach*. That is, we must have a basic understanding of why someone is lost without Christ. Basic scriptural truth teaches that we are all sinners and have gone our own way. We have the light of creation (Romans 1:19–20), the light of conscience (Romans 2:15–16), and the light of Christ (John 1:1–14) to convict us. And yet many still are lost for two primary reasons: they are bound by the god of this world, the devil, and they are blinded by him as well.

First, those without Christ are bound by the devil. Paul reminds us that it is God who "grants" repentance "so that they may know the truth, and that they may come to their senses and escape the snare of the devil, having been taken captive by him to do his will" (2 Timothy 2:25–26). The lost are bound in a stronghold of the devil himself. They are not just bound but blinded by him: "If our gospel is veiled, it is veiled to those who are perishing, whose minds the god of this age has blinded, who do not believe" (2 Corinthians 4:3–4). Therefore, to come to Christ the binding and the blinding must be broken.

It is at this point that true spiritual warfare enters the picture. The Bible reminds us that "the weapons of our warfare are not carnal but mighty in God for pulling down strongholds" (2 Corinthians 10:4). We have the spiritual authority to move through prayer into the spiritual realm and pull down strongholds of pride, procrastination, presumption, or any stronghold that may cause one to be bound or blinded. Thus, the proper approach in praying for the lost is to have an understanding of why they are lost in the first place and enter into intercessory prayer "for pulling down strongholds."

> We have the spiritual authority to move through prayer into the spiritual realm and pull down strongholds.

PRAYING WITH THE PROPER AIM

Praying for those without Christ also involves *praying with the proper aim*. Where is our aim, our focus, in praying for the lost? Many of us aim our prayers straight at the individual in question. "Lord, save Billy. Lord help him; bless him." But since he is bound and blinded by the god of this world, our aim should be at Satan himself.

We find this truth embedded throughout the New

Testament. Jesus never dealt with surface issues but went straight to the root of issues by dealing not with the problem but with the power behind it. One evening in Caesarea Philippi, Simon Peter made what has come to be known as "the great confession" by exclaiming that Jesus was indeed the promised Anointed One, the Messiah. Jesus then revealed that He would go to Jerusalem, suffer many things, and eventually be killed. Peter rebuked the thought. Jesus looked straight into his eyes and replied, "Get behind Me, Satan" (Matthew 16:23). He was not addressing Peter, but the spirit that was behind his trying to divert Jesus from the cross. Paul had a similar experience on this second missionary journey when harassed by a fortune-teller. He rebuked by speaking to the spirit within her (Acts 16:18). When praying for the lost, we should pray with the same aim in our prayers. Since Satan has bound and blinded the lost person, we aim at him in our prayers, driving him off the battlefield of God's will.

PRAYING WITH THE PROPER AUTHORITY

Finally, praying for the lost involves *praying with the proper authority*. When we pray for the lost, we stand firm on the victory that Christ has already won for us, for "the Son of God was manifested, that He might destroy the works of the devil" (1 John 3:8). Only Christ has the power to "release

those who through fear of death were all their lifetime sub-
ject to bondage" (Hebrews 2:15).

Since this is all true, my job in intercessory prayer is to
discern strongholds and enter into the spiritual battlefield
standing on the truth of Mark 3:27: "No one can enter a
strong man's house and plunder his goods, unless he first
binds the strong man." Praying for the lost is not a prayer to
persuade a reluctant God but to stand squarely against the
devil on someone's behalf. This prayer drives the devil off the
battlefield of God's will, loosing the binding and healing the
blinding, thus freeing the lost man to trust in Christ. Prayers
for the lost do not force a person to trust in Christ, but free
him to do so.

Prayer is the battlefield of the Christian experience.
Someone you know needs to know Christ. Pray for them . . .
right now . . . with the proper approach, the proper aim, and
with the proper authority given to you in and through the
Lord Jesus Christ.

CODE WORD: POLICE OFFICER

Today, when you see a police officer directing traffic in an intersection, let it remind you that as the officer stands there with raised hand to stop traffic, he or she doesn't have the power to stop those mighty machines. But the officer stands there with all the authority of the city government behind him or her. When you pray, you have no real power in and of yourself, but you pray from the platform of all the authority granted to you by Jesus Christ Himself.

CODE VERSE

The weapons of our warfare are not carnal but mighty in God for pulling down strongholds, casting down arguments . . . bringing every thought into captivity to the obedience of Christ. (2 Corinthians 10:4–5)

34 ANSWERED PRAYER

Beloved, if our heart does not condemn us, we have confidence
toward God. And whatever we ask we receive from Him,
because we keep His commandments and do those things
that are pleasing in His sight. And this is His commandment:
that we should believe on the name of His Son Jesus Christ
and love one another, as He gave us commandment.

—1 JOHN 3:21–23

*F*or our prayers to be answered, we must have a pure
heart. And, when our heart, our inner voice, does
not condemn us, it enables us to have confidence, boldness,
before God. The ability to be bold involves living in a right
relationship. Most of us in Christian leadership have experi-
enced those around us who simply did not have the boldness
to confront us, or often even to approach us. This was never
true of my own children. Our relationship created in them a
boldness to approach me regarding anything and everything
that might have been on their minds.

The apostle John is telling us that those of us in a proper
relationship with the Lord Jesus Christ have confidence
(boldness) toward God. This is because we come to Him as
children to a loving Father. We can trust Him because we
know Him.

THE MEASURE

Answered prayer is limitless. "Whatever we ask we receive from Him." That is a bold statement, but in understanding its meaning we must allow Scripture to interpret Scripture. When we do, we read, "You ask and do not receive, because you ask amiss, that you may spend it on your pleasures" (James 4:3). Proper motives that are selfless are essential in seeing our prayers answered. John went on in his first letter to say, "If we ask anything according to His will, He hears us" (1 John 5:14). Seeing the truth of asking and receiving does not simply involve selflessness but submission to the Lord's will in a matter.

One of the purposes of prayer, apart from God's glory, is that we might find ourselves on the receiving end of His grace and goodness toward us. He is a giving God and delights in doing so. What have you received from Him lately? Think about it. There is nothing more exhilarating than to watch our invisible God do visible things that only He can do in meeting our requested needs. Prayer's measure is limitless: "Whatever we ask . . ."

THE MEANS

If the measure of answered prayer is "Whatever we ask," then the means is "because we keep His commandments and do those things that are pleasing in His sight." But there is a flashing yellow light of caution here. Do not make God's answers to your prayers conditioned solely on your own obedience. Even though our two daughters obeyed me in their growing-up years, I did not necessarily give to them everything they asked of me. In some cases doing so could have led to a spoiled and self-centered child. And besides, I knew what was best for them when they did not have the experience and knowledge to know for themselves.

Is John saying here that as long as I live a good life marked by obedience that I will get anything and everything I ask from God? No. But what he is saying is that if I am keeping God's commandments, doing His will, living the Spirit-filled life, I can be confident that my life is being controlled by His Spirit, and consequently my prayer requests have been created in me by the Holy Spirit who lives in me and guides me. This was the point of Paul's teaching to the Romans when he said the Holy Spirit "helps in our weaknesses. For we do not know what we should pray for as we ought . . . He makes intercession for the saints according to the will of God" (Romans 8:26–27).

THE MANDATE

"And this is His commandment." Those five words ought to move us to the edge of our seats in anticipation of what comes next. "Believe on the name of His Son . . . [and] love one another." And there you have it. This is our mandate. As Jesus responded to the inquirer as to what was the greatest commandment in the Torah, He replied, "Love the LORD your God with all your heart, . . . and love your neighbor as yourself" (Matthew 22:37–39). Faith and love go hand in hand with answered prayer.

> Faith and love go hand in hand with answered prayer.

Believing "on the name of His Son," that is, trusting Him, is essential to seeing our prayers answered. Asking "in faith, with no doubting" is the key (James 1:6). Some wonder why they have difficulty obeying God. The answer is simple. They do not trust Him. But it is deeper than that. They do not trust Him because they do not know Him in the intimacy of a Father and child. You might ask me to do something, and I might want to know what it is before I give you a reply. But if my wife, Susie, asked me to do something, I would have no difficulty obeying her because I trust her. And I trust her because I know her. Faith, knowing Christ, leads to trusting Him, and when we trust Him we will have no problem obeying Him.

Our relationship with others around us cannot be divorced from our ability to see God answer our prayers. Jesus made this crystal clear when He said, "Whenever you stand praying, if you have anything against anyone, forgive him, that your Father in heaven may also forgive you your trespasses" (Mark 11:25). Later Peter added a word on this point regarding the husband-wife relationship as it applies to answered prayer, when he admonished husbands to live in love and honor toward their wives "that your prayers may not be hindered" (1 Peter 3:7).

What is the prayer you would most like to see answered right now? Approach Him with boldness, in faith, and rightly related to Him and others. Then, go ahead and ask.

CODE WORD: STOP SIGN

Today, when you stop at a stop sign, signaling to you that the city government erected it to command you to stop before proceeding, let it remind you that the greatest of all the commands is to love the Lord with all your heart and to love others as you love yourself.

CODE VERSE

You do not have because you do not ask. (James 4:2)

35

A PRAYER OF ACKNOWLEDGMENT

Thomas answered and said to Him, "My Lord and my God!"
—JOHN 20:28

The words of this prayer are the strongest acknowledgment of the deity of Christ to be found in all the New Testament. And they are expressed by the unlikeliest of people. Thomas earned a nickname that stuck like glue: "Doubting Thomas." Virtually every time he takes center stage in the Gospels, we find him thinking the worst or casting doubt on something or someone. Thomas saw a problem in every answer when Christ saw an answer in every problem. When Jesus got word that His friend Lazarus was dying, He told His disciples that he must go down to Judea. They tried to talk Him out of it because on their last journey these people had taken up stones to kill Him. Thomas chimed in, saying essentially, "Let's just all go and die with him" (John 11:16). In the upper room, when Jesus told them He was going to prepare a place for them, Thomas interrupted. "We do not know where You are going . . . how can we know the way?" (John 14:5). And after the resurrection his doubting reached a terrible climax. The risen Christ had appeared to the disciples, but Thomas "was not with

> "Unless I see in His hands the print of the nails . . . I will not believe."
>
> JOHN 20:25

them when Jesus came" (John 20:24). When Thomas returned, they excitedly shared the good news with him that Christ was alive. And his reply? "Unless I see in His hands the print of the nails, and put my finger into the print of the nails, and put my hand in His side, I will not believe" (v. 25).

But all that changed eight days later. Jesus returned, walked through the closed door, looked at Thomas, and said, "Reach your finger here, and look at My hands, and reach your hand here, and put it into My side. Do not be unbelieving, but believing" (v. 27). Thomas suddenly realized he did not need the evidence he thought he needed, and falling at Jesus' feet, he prayed, "My Lord and my God!" (v. 28). In that moment the worrier became the worshiper, the troubled doubter became a true disciple.

The purpose of this brief chapter is not to convince you of the resurrection. If those early believers who witnessed the risen Christ, saw Him, and sat with Him, could not convince Thomas that He was alive, I am under no illusions that in these few paragraphs I can convince you. You will never be persuaded until, like Thomas, you have a personal encounter with Him yourself and, by faith, come to the same conclusion—that indeed, He is both Lord and God.

When we pray, "My Lord," there is so much behind that acknowledgment. When Thomas prayed these two words, it was an acknowledgment that he had now received the Holy Spirit. We can be sure of this because the Bible says, "No one can say that Jesus is Lord except by the Holy Spirit" (1 Corinthians 12:3). When God manifests Himself to us in such a personal way, our natural response is, "My Lord."

Undoubtedly, one of the ways we will know our Lord in Glory is by the marks in His hands. Let us never forget that down through the corridors of the centuries walks One who by merely raising His hands reminds us of His claim on us. And those of us who have placed our own hand in His nailed-scarred hand have, like Thomas, bowed before Him and said, "My Lord."

There is also an acknowledgment behind those words "my God." This is the most obvious place in the Gospels when someone began to own Jesus Christ as his God. How marvelous is the grace of God. Doubting Thomas was the one who gave the clearest, boldest, and most pointed acknowledgment to the deity of Christ in all the Bible when he exclaimed, "My Lord *and* my God." It was Peter, who failed so often, who made the great confession. It was Paul who after having persecuted the early church, became the Apostle to the Gentiles, and took the gospel across the Mediterranean world in one generation. And so it is that the biggest skeptic among the band of twelve, Doubting Thomas, was the one to say not just "my Lord" but to add the acknowledgment "my God."

Our Lord had been dropping hints of His deity all along the way of John's gospel. In chapter 1, John said, "In the beginning was the Word, and the Word was with God, and the Word was God . . . and the Word became flesh and dwelt among us" (John 1:1, 14). In John 10:30 Jesus had said that He and the Father were "one." And in John 14:9, on the eve of His crucifixion, He confessed that those who had seen Him had "seen the Father." Jesus was none other than the long-awaited Messiah. All that is behind this prayer, "My Lord and my God."

Jesus looked at Thomas and said, "Thomas, because you have seen Me, you have believed. Blessed are those who have not seen and yet have believed" (John 20:29). Thomas was insistent on seeing the risen Christ. Jesus granted his request, and thus Thomas believed. But the Lord pointed out that a greater blessing awaits those who would never see with their eyes but who would believe with their hearts. I have never seen Him, but as a seventeen-year-old, I believed and joined Thomas, saying, "My Lord and my God."

If only the Lord could step out of the pages of this book, look into your eyes, and say, "Behold My hands; bring your sin and put it on Me; bring your burdens and put them on Me; bring your frustrations and pour them out on Me;

bring your worries and let Me bear them." The good news is He is with you this moment, and when you see Him as Thomas did, you too will suddenly realize that all the proof you thought you needed doesn't matter, and you will bow to acknowledge, "My Lord and my God."

CODE WORD: SCAR

Today, when you notice a scar on your body that may have been brought about by an injury or surgery long ago, let it remind you that there is One who is standing before you this very moment who by merely raising His hands and revealing His scars shows you how much He loves you and the claim He has on your life.

CODE VERSE

"Have I been with you so long, and yet have you not known me, Philip? He who has seen Me has seen the Father; so how can you say, 'Show us the Father'?" (John 14:9)

36 PRAYER AND THE WILL OF GOD

"Father, if it is Your will, take this cup away from Me;
nevertheless not My will, but Yours, be done."

—LUKE 22:42

*A*s the shadows fell on Gethsemane, we find our Lord so anguished in prayer that He began to literally sweat drops of blood. His passion was focused on accomplishing the Father's will for His life. Earlier, He pointedly declared to His disciples, "I have come down from heaven, not to do My own will, but the will of Him who sent me" (John 6:38). Now, just hours before He would hang on a Roman cross, bearing the weight of the world's sin, it was this same desire that consumed Him. That is, "Not My will, but Yours, be done."

God has a perfect plan and purpose for each of us. King David believed this and revealed his confidence that God would not conceal it. He said, "You will show me the path of life; in Your presence is fullness of joy; at Your right hand are pleasures forevermore" (Psalm 16:11). The Lord Jesus is more interested in us finding His will for us than we are ourselves.

There are certain issues related to God's will that need

no prayer or searching. For example, Jesus said, "This is the will of Him who sent Me, that everyone who sees the Son and believes in Him may have everlasting life" (John 6:40). This is the explicit will of the Father. But what about some of those other issues, those crossroads in life that demand our attention and an eventual decision? How do we discover God's will? We pray. We ask and we make sure of three important factors that enable us to find the will of God for our lives and do it.

BE SURE YOU KNOW THE SAVIOR

If we are in pursuit of the will of God in a matter, it stands to reason that we first need to know Him as a personal Lord and Savior. The apostle Paul made this truth crystal clear when he said, "This is good and acceptable in the sight of God our Savior, who desires all men to be saved and to come to the knowledge of the truth" (1 Timothy 2:3–4).

The initial step in finding God's will is to pray and open your heart to Him. Without a saving knowledge of Christ and His abiding life within, it is impossible to discern the things of God. These matters, as the Scriptures say, are "spiritually discerned" (1 Corinthians 2:14). So the place to begin to find the will of God is to be sure you know Him in the intimacy of Father and child, and to know Him is eternal life.

BE SURE YOU KNOW THE SPIRIT

> Once you place your trust in Christ alone for your salvation, the Holy Spirit comes to take up residency in your very life.

Once you place your trust in Christ alone for your salvation, the Holy Spirit comes to take up residency in your very life, empowering you for service and helping you bear witness with the Spirit of God. Paul admonished us to "not be unwise, but understand what the will of the Lord is. And do not be drunk with wine . . . but be filled with the Spirit" (Ephesians 5:17–18).

What begins to happen when we know Christ as our Savior and are being filled daily with His Spirit? He becomes our Teacher and will "guide [us] into all truth" (John 16:13). As we yield more of ourselves through prayer to the Holy Spirit, He promises to lead us in discerning God's will for our lives.

BE SURE YOU KNOW THE SCRIPTURE

A knowledge of biblical truth is essential in finding the will of God for our lives. God will never lead us to do anything that is contrary to what we find in His Word. No wonder Paul's challenge to us is to "let the word of Christ dwell in you richly in all wisdom" (Colossians 3:16). When we know Christ, are being controlled by His Spirit, and are abiding in His Word, He "will show [us] the path of life" (Psalm 16:11).

As we pray to discover God's will in a particular matter in our own lives, there are some practical steps to find it. The first key is *desire*. God will not call you to an endeavor without first putting a desire in your heart to do it (Psalm 37). When a person is abiding in the Spirit and immersed in the Scripture, the desires of his heart will have been implanted there by God Himself. He gives us those desires that arise in our hearts. But a desire in and of itself is not necessarily His will for us. Secondly, the desire must be accompanied by an *opportunity*. Then if we have a desire coupled with an opportunity, we are to keep walking and trust Him to shut the door if it is not His will for us.

God has no desire to veil His will from you. He is more desirous of you finding it, and walking in it, than you could ever possibly be yourself. Yes, He has a wonderful plan for your life . . . right now . . . and He longs to make His will known to you. He knows you intimately. He knows your name. He knows your e-mail address. He has even numbered the hairs of your head. If He sees a sparrow when it falls from the sky, how much more does He care for you (Matthew 10:30)? Join Jesus in praying, "Lord, not my will . . . but Yours be done."

CODE WORD: GARDEN

Today, when you see a garden or drive past a beauti-
fully manicured lawn with well-placed flower beds, let it
remind you that it was in a garden that Jesus prayed, "Not
My will, but Yours, be done." And make that your earnest
prayer throughout this day.

CODE VERSE

*Do not be conformed to this world, but be transformed by the
renewing of your mind, that you may prove what is that good
and acceptable and perfect will of God. (Romans 12:2)*

37   WATCH AND PRAY

*He came to the disciples and found them sleeping, and
said to Peter, "What! Could you not watch with Me one
hour? Watch and pray, lest you enter into temptation.
The spirit indeed is willing, but the flesh is weak."*
—MATTHEW 26:40–41

*F*or three years Jesus had spent virtually every hour
with His small, handpicked band of brothers. The
disciples had listened as He spoke the most profound words
of truth and life ever uttered. They had watched as He perfectly practiced everything He taught and preached. They
had been there when He healed the sick, raised the dead,
and walked on the surface of the waters of Galilee. He had
poured His life into them night and day, preparing them to
take the gospel of His life, death, burial, and resurrection to
the entire world. Now, His time had come. The midnight
hour had finally arrived. In a matter of hours, He would be
hanging from a Roman cross, despised and rejected. Into
the darkness of Gethsemane's garden He took with Him the
inner three: Peter, James, and John. They saw clearly in His
face that He "began to be sorrowful and deeply distressed"
(Matthew 26:37). He turned to them and verbalized His feelings: "My soul is exceedingly sorrowful, even to death. Stay

here and watch with Me" (v. 38). Put yourself in their place. After all you had seen in His life and heard from His lips, you would be eager to stand with Him in such a moment. In this, His hour of greatest need, it was a simple request: "Stay here and watch with Me."

Knowing His death was but hours away, Jesus went a few steps from them before dropping to His knees on the ground and praying, "O My Father, if it is possible, let this cup pass from Me; nevertheless, not as I will, but as You will" (v. 39). After a while, Jesus returned to the disciples and found them sound asleep. It is hard to believe. They were asleep . . . and in His hour of greatest need. Then out of His lips came this penetrating and piercing question: "What! Could you not watch with Me one hour?"

Jesus looked into Peter's face and asked this question. The same Simon Peter who one day would rise to become the undisputed leader of the Jerusalem church. The question was also directed at James, one of the "Sons of Thunder" and the first apostle who would not long after this meet his own martyr's death. And John, who years later would be exiled to Patmos, where he would receive the Revelation, heard our Lord ask, "Could you not watch with Me one hour?" I am certain that upon hearing this, these three, trained in the Hebrew Scriptures, thought of the words of Isaiah, who, speaking of the watchmen placed along the walls of

Jerusalem, revealed how they "shall never hold their peace day or night" (Isaiah 62:6).

During this hour of prayer, Peter, James, and John had the opportunity to provide their Lord with physical security as well as spiritual security. They could have been on watch to alert Jesus of anyone entering Gethsemane that night with intentions to do Him harm. They could have prayed for Him, for strength and courage to meet the defining moment at hand. They could have comforted Him in His time of sorrow and distress. But they did none of this. They dozed off into a deep sleep.

There was a note of astonishment, even disbelief, in Jesus' voice when He asked them this question. First came the exclamation mark, "What!" "What! What is this? I simply asked you to watch and pray. Could you not do this for just an hour?" They had just come from the holy ground of the upper room, partaking of the bread and the wine, hearing our Lord describing His broken body and shed blood. Now came the stinging question, "What! Could you not watch with Me one hour?"

Before we are too quick to point our own fingers of accusation in their direction, this question is aimed at us as well. There are times in our own

> "What! What is this? I simply asked you to watch and pray. Could you not do this for just an hour?"
>
> MATTHEW 26:40, PARAPHRASE

Christian experience when our working takes the place of our watching. In these moments Jesus whispers these same words to us: "Watch and pray, lest you enter into temptation. The spirit is willing, but the flesh is weak."

Listen again to this question: "Could you not watch with Me one hour?" Isn't it time that we who name Jesus as our Savior and Lord take seriously this question as though we were there that night? When, in our day, and in so many places, the heart of the church is turned to stone and many pulpits are simply dispensaries of human thought; when many of our education systems have become citadels of anti-Christian propaganda and blatant Marxism; when the media at every hand constantly calls our children to lifestyles of godlessness; when many modern disciples increasingly tolerate a dying civilization; isn't it time to hear clearly this question of Jesus in our day: "What! Could you not watch with Me one hour?" And then, in deep conviction, begin to pray, "Oh, that You would rend the heavens! That You would come down!" (Isaiah 64:1).

Yes, before we become too critical of this slumbering trio, we should use today to examine our own hearts. Despite our sometimes-willing spirits, we too are so often weak in the flesh when it comes to the call to "watch and pray." Keep watch today. "Let him who thinks he stands take heed lest he fall" (1 Corinthians 10:12). And as you watch, remember to pray.

CODE WORD: CLOCK

Today when you look at a clock as it ticks off the seconds, minutes, and hours of your day, let it be a reminder of this question that comes to you as it did to the three in the garden: "Could you not watch with Me one hour?" May it motivate you to "watch and pray lest you enter into temptation."

CODE VERSE

"I have set watchmen on your walls, O Jerusalem; they shall never hold their peace day or night. You who make mention of the Lord, do not keep silent; and give Him no rest till He establishes and till He makes Jerusalem a praise in the earth." (Isaiah 62:6–7)

38 PRAYERS FROM THE CROSS

"Father, forgive them, for they do not know what they do."

—LUKE 23:34

"My God, My God, why have You forsaken Me?"

—MATTHEW 27:46

"Father, 'into Your hands I commit My spirit.'"

—LUKE 23:46

*T*he famous last words spoken by dying men and women are always memorable and often impressive. Jesus of Nazareth's last words were spoken from an instrument of execution. From a Roman cross He spoke seven times. His first, middle, and last words spoken were all prayers, prayers that speak volumes to you and me in this dispensation of grace in which we now live.

A strange darkness enveloped the earth in the middle of the day as Christ hung suspended between earth and heaven. Before the darkness He spoke three times saying, "Father, forgive them . . . Today you will be with Me in Paradise" (Luke 23:34, 43); "Woman, behold your Son" (John 19:26). Then, from the darkness, came the strangest of all His last words, "My God, why have You forsaken Me?" After the darkness, and in rapid succession, came the words "I thirst" (John 19:28) . . . "It is finished" (v. 30) . . . "Father, into Your hands I commit My spirit" (Luke 23:46).

A COMPASSIONATE PRAYER

From the cross Jesus offered a *compassionate prayer*. Before He ever said that He was thirsty, before He ever delivered His mother into John's care, before He ever spoke hope to the dying thief, He prayed . . . and He prayed for those who were killing Him. "Father, forgive them, for they do not know what they do."

The tense of this expression in the New Testament indicates that this was not a single prayer shot at random from dying lips, but one that was repeated over and over and over. When He arrived at Calvary, those standing there could hear, "Father, forgive them." When the soldiers shoved Him to the ground, they heard, "Father, forgive them." When the executioner drove the spikes into His hands and feet, he heard, "Father, forgive them." When the cross was lifted and dropped with a thud in the ground, those looking up from below heard, "Father, forgive them." No one knows how many times that prayer penetrated the heavens that day. Jesus died loving others and praying this compassionate prayer on their behalf.

Earlier on a grassy green hillside in Galilee He had said to His followers, "Love your enemies . . . bless them . . . do

> What He had preached so eloquently on a mountain in Galilee, He now practiced on the grim hill of Golgotha.

good to them . . . pray for them" (Matthew 5:44, paraphrase). On another occasion, when queried about how many times we should forgive, He replied, "Seventy times seven" (Matthew 18:22). He was teaching us all a valuable life lesson. What He had preached so eloquently on a mountain in Galilee, He now practiced on the grim hill of Golgotha. This prayer is recorded for all posterity in order that we might know the power and liberating effect that forgiving others can have on and in our own lives.

A COMPLETED PROPHECY

The second petition from the cross came in the form of a *completed prophecy*. Total darkness enveloped the earth, followed by an eerie silence, and then a loud shout penetrated the silence and darkness—"My God, My God, why have You forsaken Me?" Some say after three hours of hanging on the cross Jesus had become delirious. But don't believe that. What motivated these prophetic words from Psalm 22 now offered in a passionate prayer? Does a loving Father ever forsake His own?

This mystery can only be understood by again letting Scripture itself interpret Scripture. Habakkuk reveals the truth that the Father's eyes "cannot look on wickedness [sin]" (Habakkuk 1:13). In Isaiah 53:6 we are reminded that God laid on Christ the sins of us all. And Paul added that God made Christ, "who knew no sin to be sin for us" (2 Corinthians 5:21). Now, since a holy God cannot look on sin, and since Jesus took all our sin in His own body on the cross, the Light turned away, and darkness ensued for that period of time when Jesus became what we are so that we could become what He is—free from sin. He was forsaken as He bore our sin so that we might never be forsaken.

A CONFIDENT PROFESSION

Our Lord's final prayer was a *confident profession.* "Father, 'into Your hands I commit My spirit.'" Now, when it was all over, Jesus made this confident profession. And note: it is His Spirit that is placed in the hands of God. The Bible tells us that you and I are made up of spirit, soul, and body. In our culture we are so body conscious. We tan it, tone it, train it, trim it, and some of us even tuck it. We spend the majority of our time focused on that part of us that will one day go back to dust. And sadly, too many of us spend too little time on that part of us that will live as long as God lives, our spirit.

As a pastor I have stood at the open graves of multiplied hundreds of people across the years, rich and poor, young and old, educated and uneducated, and people of different races. The common denominator is the only thing that ultimately matters is whether at the door of death we can pray with Him, "Father, 'into Your hands I commit my spirit.'"

As this chapter comes to a close, we turn away from Calvary, but the shadow of the cross will always loom over us. There are prayers to be prayed that we first heard there. First, can you join Jesus in praying this compassionate prayer: "Father, forgive them"? Perhaps there is someone in your own experience you have never forgiven. That emotion has lingered for months, perhaps years. Let it go. Forgive them. Set them free. And in so doing, you will set yourself free. Jesus' second prayer from the cross is one you will never have to pray: "Why have You forsaken me?" Because Jesus was for that moment forsaken, you will never be. In fact, you have His promise: "I will never leave you nor forsake you" (Hebrews 13:5). Finally, every day is a gift. So make sure you are always ready to make this your prayer: "Father, 'into Your hands I commit my spirit.'" When that moment comes for you, you will not be leaving home, but going home!

CODE WORD: FACE

Today when you look at your face in the mirror to apply your makeup or to shave, take a good, long look. Age has an effect on all of us because our bodies are dying a bit every day. Let it remind you to feed your spirit today and nurture that part of you that is going to live as long as God lives. You are a spirit, you have a soul (a seat of emotions), and you simply live in a body.

CODE VERSE

God is Spirit, and those who worship Him must
worship in spirit and truth. (John 4:24)

39 A PRAYER OF AFFIRMATION

I thank my God, making mention of you always in my prayers,
hearing of your love and faith which you have toward the Lord Jesus
and toward all the saints, that the sharing of your faith may become
effective by the acknowledgment of every good thing which is in you
in Christ Jesus. For we have great joy and consolation in your love,
because the hearts of the saints have been refreshed by you, brother.
—PHILEMON VV. 4–7

$\mathcal{P}$aul wrote these words from his prison cell in Rome to
his friend Philemon in Colossae, whom he had earlier
won to a saving faith in Christ. Later, in this letter, he asked
Philemon to do a hard thing: to forgive and take back his
runaway servant, Onesimus, "no longer as a slave but . . . a
beloved brother" (Philemon v. 16). But first, the great apostle
wanted his friend to know that he was praying for him and
thanking God for him. Then he reached out through pen
and paper to give Philemon a pat on the back as he said he
had "great joy and consolation" in his love and affirmed that
"the hearts of the saints have been refreshed" by the many
acts of this good man (v. 7).

Prayers of affirmation should be high on the list of our
own prayers as we, like Paul, intercede for others with thanksgiving, "making mention of you always in our prayers." In

this simple mention of his prayers for Philemon, Paul laid out for us several principles that should characterize our own prayers for our friends.

OUR PRAYERS SHOULD HAVE APPRECIATION

When praying for others, our prayers should contain the element of *appreciation*. Paul wrote, "I thank my God, making mention of you always in my prayers." He was not bashful about letting Philemon know he was the object of his prayers and that when he prayed for him, he always did so with thanksgiving. And why? Because he had heard of the "love and faith" Philemon had exhibited equally to all the saints.

It is most encouraging and affirming when we let our friends know we are praying for them with thanksgiving and for a specific reason. Make sure your prayers begin with appreciation, and thanksgiving, which the psalmist says is the gateway into the throne room of prayer (Psalm 100:4).

> It is most encouraging and affirming when we let our friends know we are praying for them.

OUR PRAYERS SHOULD HAVE AUTHENTICATION

When praying for others, our prayers should also contain the element of *authentication*. Not only had Paul heard of

Philemon's "faith and love," but it was authenticated by the "sharing of his faith." In his prayer Paul was challenging his friend to be active, not reactive, in expressing his faith.

Can you imagine a major event in life, like getting married, having a first child, winning a championship of some kind, and never having a desire to talk about it or share it with anyone? Is it even possible that the Creator of this entire universe could forgive you of every sin you have ever committed and come to take up residency in your very life without you having a desire to share it with someone? Paul prayed that the "sharing" of Philemon's faith might become effective and thereby authenticate the gospel of Jesus Christ in the process.

OUR PRAYERS SHOULD HAVE ADMIRATION

When praying for others, our prayers should contain not just the elements of appreciation and authentication but of *admiration*. Paul wanted Philemon to know that his prayers for him brought him personal "joy and consolation" because of the love that permeated Philemon's very being. What exactly was it about Philemon that was so admirable? It was his love. And where did it originate? From his personal faith in Jesus Christ. His giving of himself to others brought "great joy" and encouragement to the imprisoned apostle miles away in a Roman prison cell.

There are some people around us who go for months without ever hearing a word of admiration from a spouse, a boss, or any number of others with whom they are in contact. Try it this week. Reach out with a word to a server at a restaurant, a cashier in the grocery line, or any one of scores of others with whom you will engage. Praying for others with an attitude of admiration has a liberating effect.

OUR PRAYERS SHOULD HAVE AFFIRMATION

Finally, when praying for others, make sure you incorporate the element of *affirmation*. Paul revealed that one of the motivations behind his prayers was that "the hearts of the saints have been refreshed" by his friend Philemon. Affirmation is the greatest motivating factor in life. Every child needs to know Mom and Dad believe in them. Every student needs to know the teacher believes in them. Every athlete needs to know the coach believes in them.

And, when you are affirming someone, make sure it is personal. Don't send someone else to give a pat on the back. Do it yourself. Make sure it is present. Affirming someone for something that happened years ago doesn't mean as much as something in the now. Make sure it is pointed. That is, make it specific like Paul did. Words of affirmation couched in garbled linguistics don't get very far. And make sure it is passionate, that it comes from your heart with authenticity. I don't know about you, but I can go a long while on one good and genuine compliment and word of affirmation.

You may be saying, "I wish I had someone praying for me like that." Instead, why don't you say, "I am going to start praying for my friends like that"? You might just find the Bible is true when it says we reap what we sow (Galatians 6:7).

Look at Jesus. He went around affirming people—a woman at a well . . . a woman taken in adultery . . . another in Bethany with an alabaster box . . . and to a thief on a Roman cross beside Him, to whom He reached out with a pat on the back to say, "Today, you will be with Me in Paradise" (Luke 23:43). When you pray, thank God as you "make mention" of your friends in prayer. And then put action to your prayers by letting them know you are praying for them, and encourage them with a pat on the back, a word of affirmation. Someone you know is waiting for just that.

CODE WORD: SWEETENER

Today, if you use an artificial sweetener in your coffee or tea, or see one on a restaurant table, let it be a reminder to you that affirmation must be authentic and not artificial. Then give someone you know a sincere pat on the back. It can change the way they think about themselves.

CODE VERSE

"Woman, where are those accusers of yours? Has no one condemned you?" She said, "No one, Lord." And Jesus said to her, "Neither do I condemn you; go and sin no more." (John 8:10–11)

40 THE LAST PRAYER OF THE BIBLE

Even so, come, Lord Jesus!

—REVELATION 22:20

*I*mmediately preceding this last recorded prayer in the Bible, prayed by the aged John on the island of Patmos, Jesus shares the last promise of the Bible. After His earthly mission was done, our Lord ascended back into heaven from the Mount of Olives in full view of His followers, who "looked steadfastly toward heaven as He went up" (Acts 1:10). Immediately two angels appeared, saying, "Men of Galilee, why do you stand gazing up into heaven? This same Jesus, who was taken up from you into heaven, will so come in like manner as you saw Him go into heaven" (v. 11).

Now, on the last page of the Bible, after sixty-six books, 1,189 chapters, 31,103 verses, and almost one million written words, Jesus, the Author Himself, closes this Book with this same theme. He promises to come back again, saying, "Surely I am coming quickly" (Revelation 22:20). And each and every generation of believers since that day has been looking for His promised return, our "blessed hope . . . [His] glorious appearing" (Titus 2:13). As John records these words for all posterity, he blurts out the last prayer recorded in all of sacred Scripture—"Even so, come, Lord Jesus!"

THE LAST PROMISE OF THE BIBLE

There are almost eight thousand promises God gives to us in the Bible. But this promise—"Surely, I am coming quickly"—yet to be fulfilled, will mark the climax of human history. The Bible holds the promises of three major comings. First, the coming of the promised Messiah, born of a virgin in the obscure and small village of Bethlehem. He came . . . and "dwelt among us" (John 1:14). For thirty-three years He showed us a picture of true love.

The second promised coming is of the Holy Spirit, foretold especially by the prophet Joel (Joel 2:28). This coming has also been fulfilled. On the day of Pentecost the Holy Spirit came to indwell believers, never to leave us, empowering us for service in God's advancing kingdom. When we put our faith and trust in Christ, His Spirit comes to take up residency within us.

The only promised coming yet to be fulfilled is the promise of Christ that He will come again to receive us "to Himself so that where He is we may be also" (John 14:3, paraphrased). Just as certain as He came the first time, He is coming the second time, not as a suffering servant but as the King of all kings and the Lord of all lords, bringing with Him a new kingdom of perfect peace.

> The only promised coming
> yet to be fulfilled is the
> promise of Christ that
> He will come again.

THE LAST PRAYER
OF THE BIBLE

Having heard this amazing promise from the Savior's own lips,
John's first impulse was to burst
out in prayer—"Even so . . . just
like You promised . . . come . . . and don't delay . . . come
now, come quickly." Just five recorded words in his actual
prayer—"Even so, come, Lord Jesus!" Often the most powerful prayers are the shortest ones. Behind the words of this
prayer, John, the beloved disciple, is anticipating the glory of
the Lord's return, which will usher in a new age of peace, a
millennial reign of Christ on this earth, followed by an eternity with Him in heaven where time will be no more.

Our world searches for peace but never seems able to
find it. We seek it at international peace tribunals, so often
ignorant of the fact that peace cannot be found there until it
is found on a national level. Of course peace on the streets of
our nation cannot be found unless it is found on an individual, state level. This, of course, is impossible without peace
being procured on a city-by-city level. This is impossible in
my city, and yours, until we have peace on a neighborhood
level, which cannot happen without having peace on our
blocks. Peace can never be achieved in a block until we have
peace in the home. Peace cannot happen in my home until

there is peace in my own heart. And peace will never come to my heart unless I have found Jesus' peace, which comes only by knowing Him as my personal Lord and Savior.

Jesus is coming again to bring a true and lasting peace among us. Before you close the pages of this devotional journey, join John and make this your prayer today and every day: "Even so, come, Lord Jesus!"

CODE WORD: NEWS

Today, when you read the news, finding all sorts of trouble and unrest at home and around the world, let it be a reminder that there is a better day coming. Allow the bad news to cause you to remember there is good news, and let it motivate you to pray, "Even so, come, Lord Jesus!"

CODE VERSE

"I go to prepare a place for you. And . . . I will come again and receive you to Myself; that where I am, there you may be also." (John 14:2–3)

EPILOGUE

*I*t may be that while you have been journeying through these pages, God's Spirit has been nudging you to put your faith and trust in Christ for the forgiveness of your sin in order to receive the gift of eternal life. After all, heaven is God's personal and free gift to you. It cannot be earned; neither is it ever deserved. We are all sinners, and each and every one of us has fallen short of God's perfect standard for our lives. Yes, God is a God of love, but He is also a God of justice and, therefore, must punish sin. This is where Jesus steps in. He is the holy and sinless God-man who came to take your own sins on Himself and to die on the cross in your place as punishment for those sins. But just knowing this fact it not enough. You must transfer your trust from your own human effort to Christ alone, placing your faith in Him, and in Him alone.

If you would like to receive this free gift of eternal life, it is yours for the asking. Paul, quoting the prophet Joel, said, "Whoever calls on the name of the LORD shall be saved" (Romans 10:13). Join Peter in his prayer on the Sea of Galilee. Say it: "Lord, save me!" (Matthew 14:30). The following is a suggested prayer you can pray, right now, from your own heart, no matter where you are.

Dear Lord Jesus,

I know I have sinned. I know that, in and of myself, I do not deserve eternal life. Please forgive me for my sin. Thank You for taking my sin on Your own body and dying on the cross on my behalf and in my place. I trust in You as the only One who can save me from an eternity of being separated from a holy God. Come into my life. Lord, save me. I accept Your free and gracious offer of forgiveness, abundant life, and eternal life with You. Thank You, Lord, for coming into my life this very moment as my very own personal Lord and Savior.

A simple prayer cannot save you. But Jesus can—and will. If this prayer has expressed the desire of your heart, you can now claim the promise Jesus made to those who believe in Him: "Most assuredly . . . he who believes in Me has everlasting life" (John 6:47).

You can now join millions of Christ's followers in praying with Thomas, "My Lord and my God!" (John 20:28). Now, what good is good news if you don't share it? Tell someone of your newfound faith in Him.

MISSION:DIGNITY

*A*ll the author's royalties and any additional proceeds from the Code series (including *The Prayer
Code*) go to the support of Mission:Dignity, a ministry that
enables thousands of retired ministers (and in most cases,
their widows) who are living near the poverty level to live
out their days with dignity and security. Many of them spent
their ministries in small churches that were unable to provide
adequately for their retirement. They also lived in church-
owned parsonages and had to vacate them upon their voca-
tional retirement as well. Mission:Dignity tangibly shows
these good and godly servants they are not forgotten and will
be cared for in their declining years.

All the expenses for this ministry are paid out of an
endowment that has already been raised. Consequently, anyone who gives to Mission:Dignity can be assured that every
cent of their gift goes straight to one of these precious saints
in need.

Find out more by visiting www.missiondignity.org, or call,
toll-free, 877-888-9409.

ABOUT THE AUTHOR

O. S. Hawkins, former pastor of the First Baptist Church in Dallas, Texas, has served as president/CEO of GuideStone Financial Resources since 1997. GuideStone is the largest Christian-screened mutual fund in the world, with assets of over $20 billion dollars. He is the bestselling author of the Code series of devotional books, which have sold more than two million copies. He is a graduate of Texas Christian University (BBA) and Southwestern Baptist Theological Seminary (MDiv; PhD).

DRAW CLOSER TO GOD

*Y*ou'll understand Jesus' presence in the Old Testament in a new way as you journey with Pastor O. S. Hawkins through the Bible in *The Bible Code*. As Jesus revealed to the two disciples on the road to Emmaus, He can be found "in all the Scriptures" (Luke 24:27). And as we learn to find Jesus in every verse, we realize His constant presence in our lives as well.

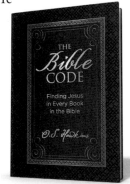

ISBN: 978-1-4002-1780-9

One hundred percent of the author's royalties and proceeds go to support Mission:Dignity—a ministry providing support for impoverished retired pastors and missionaries.